Jean Racine's
Cantiques spirituels

RECENT RESEARCHES IN MUSIC

A-R Editions publishes seven series of critical editions, spanning the history of Western music, American music, and oral traditions.

RECENT RESEARCHES IN THE MUSIC OF THE MIDDLE AGES AND EARLY RENAISSANCE
  Charles M. Atkinson, general editor

RECENT RESEARCHES IN THE MUSIC OF THE RENAISSANCE
  James Haar, general editor

RECENT RESEARCHES IN THE MUSIC OF THE BAROQUE ERA
  Steven Saunders, general editor

RECENT RESEARCHES IN THE MUSIC OF THE CLASSICAL ERA
  Neal Zaslaw, general editor

RECENT RESEARCHES IN THE MUSIC OF THE NINETEENTH AND EARLY TWENTIETH CENTURIES
  Rufus Hallmark, general editor

RECENT RESEARCHES IN AMERICAN MUSIC
  John M. Graziano, general editor

RECENT RESEARCHES IN THE ORAL TRADITIONS OF MUSIC
  Philip V. Bohlman, general editor

Each edition in *Recent Researches* is devoted to works by a single composer or to a single genre. The content is chosen for its high quality and historical importance and is edited according to the scholarly standards that govern the making of all reliable editions.

For information on establishing a standing order to any of our series, or for editorial guidelines on submitting proposals, please contact:

A-R Editions, Inc.
Middleton, Wisconsin

800 736-0070 (North American book orders)
608 836-9000 (phone)
608 831-8200 (fax)
http://www.areditions.com

RECENT RESEARCHES IN THE MUSIC OF THE BAROQUE ERA, 178

Jean Racine's *Cantiques spirituels*

Musical Settings by Moreau, Lalande, Collasse, Marchand, Duhalle, and Bousset

Edited by Deborah Kauffman

A-R Editions, Inc.
Middleton, Wisconsin

To my husband and son, Jonathan and Benjamin
Bellman, and in loving memory of my sister,
Kathleen Kauffman.

Performance parts are available from the publisher.

A-R Editions, Inc., Middleton, Wisconsin
© 2012 by A-R Editions, Inc.

All rights reserved. No part of this book may be reproduced
or transmitted in any form by any electronic or mechanical
means (including photocopying, recording, or information
storage and retrieval) without permission in writing from
the publisher.

The purchase of this edition does not convey the right to
perform it in public, nor to make a recording of it for any
purpose. Such permission must be obtained in advance
from the publisher.

A-R Editions is pleased to support scholars and performers
in their use of *Recent Researches* material for study or performance.
Please visit our website (www.areditions.com) to
apply for permission to perform, record, or otherwise reuse
the material in this publication.

Printed in the United States of America

ISBN 978-0-89579-729-2
ISSN 0484-0828

♾ The paper used in this publication meets the minimum
requirements of the American National Standard for
Information Sciences—Permanence of Paper for Printed
Library Materials, ANSI Z39.48-1992.

Contents

Acknowledgments   vii

Introduction   ix

   Jean Racine's *Cantiques spirituels*   ix
   The *Cantique spirituel* Tradition   x
   The Composers   xi
   The Music   xii
   Notes on Performance   xiv
   Notes   xvi

Texts and Translations   xviii
   Notes   xxii

Plates   xxiii

Jean-Baptiste Moreau and Michel-Richard de Lalande, *Cantiques chantez devant le Roy*

   Les méchants m'ont vanté (Moreau)   3
   Mon Dieu, quelle guerre cruelle! (Moreau)   12
   Quel charme vainqueur du monde (Moreau)   15
   Heureux qui, de la sagesse (Lalande)   21

Pascal Collasse, *Cantiques spirituels, mis en musique* (1695)

   Les méchants m'ont vanté   31
   Heureux qui, de la sagesse   63
   Mon Dieu, quelle guerre cruelle!   80
   Quel charme vainqueur du monde   89

Jean-Noël Marchand, *Cantiques spirituels faits par M Racine*

   Les méchants m'ont vanté   115
   Heureux qui, de la sagesse   143
   Mon Dieu, quelle guerre cruelle!   165
   Quel charme vainqueur du monde   173

Settings of Individual *Cantiques spirituels*

   Duhalle, *Heureux qui, de la sagesse*   196
   Duhalle, *Mon Dieu, quelle guerre cruelle!*   204
   Jean-Baptiste de Bousset, "Hélas! en guerre avec moi-même"   208

Critical Report   209

   Library Sigla   209
   Sources   209
   Editorial Methods   210
   Critical Notes   211
   Notes   213

Appendix: Alternative Settings by Moreau and Lalande of Individual Stanzas
    "Que je vois de Vertus" (Moreau, stanza 6 of *Les méchants m'ont vanté*)   216
    "L'Amour sur tous les dons" (Moreau, stanza 12 of *Les méchants m'ont vanté*)   217
    "L'un tout esprit, et tout céleste" (Moreau, stanza 2 of *Mon Dieu, quelle guerre cruelle!*)   219
    "Ô grâce, ô rayon salutaire" (Moreau, stanza 4 of *Mon Dieu, quelle guerre cruelle!*)   220
    "Infortunés que nous sommes" (Lalande, stanza 3 of *Heureux qui, de la sagesse*)   222
    "Pour trouver un bien fragile" (Lalande, stanza 4 of *Heureux qui, de la sagesse*)   224
    "De nos attentats injustes" (Lalande, stanza 5 of *Heureux qui, de la sagesse*)   226
    Critical Notes   228

Acknowledgments

I extend my heartfelt thanks to Dr. Christopher Braider, Professor of French and Comparative Literature at the University of Colorado, Boulder, for his invaluable help with the translation of Racine's beautiful poetry. My good friend, Dr. Cécile Davy-Rigaux, at the Institut de recherche sur le patrimoine musical en France, was kind enough to help me connect with scholars in France, including Dr. Thierry Favier, who provided me with the location of the pieces found in the appendix. Mme Maryse Viviand and Mr Yann Sordet of the Bibliothèque Sainte-Geneviève helped me obtain reproductions of the *Cantiques* by Duhalle. I also extend my thanks to the editorial staff at A-R Editions, who caught things before they fell through the cracks.

The Bibliothèque nationale de France and the Bibliothèque Sainte-Geneviève graciously allowed the use of materials in their collections.

Introduction

Jean Racine's *Cantiques spirituels*

Jean Racine has long been recognized as one of the great writers of classical French tragedy. His biographers show him to be an elusive character, with family roots in the Jansenist religious community, an early career in the theater, and a seemingly sober mature life as a courtier and royal historiographer. He was baptized on 22 December 1639, and was a pupil at the controversial Jansenist convent of Port-Royal, where his aunt, Agnès de Sainte-Thècle, served as superior. Racine's storied career as a dramatist was compressed into a very short period of time. His first work, *La Thébaïde*, was produced by Molière in 1663, and he became widely known with *Andromaque* in 1667. His masterpiece, *Phèdre*, appeared in 1677, but it drew the criticism of a cabal aligned against the author and eventually led to the end of his theatrical career. Nevertheless, Racine continued to oversee reprintings, editions, and some revivals of his works. He took up a court position with his friend Nicolas Boileau as historiographer to Louis XIV, solidifying his close connection with the court, even accompanying the king on campaigns of war.

Racine wrote his four *Cantiques spirituels* between September and December 1694.[1] The poems are spiritual texts in French, based on selections from the Old and New Testaments, and seem to have been specifically written to be set to music;[2] their title itself suggests this, as the *cantique spirituel* was already a familiar musical genre. The poems were probably the result of a commission by Madame de Maintenon, the second wife of Louis XIV, for whom Racine had already fulfilled two commissions for the girls of the Maison royale de Saint-Louis at Saint-Cyr: the two *tragédies chrétiennes*, *Esther* and *Athalie*. Indeed, the first musical settings of Racine's *Cantiques spirituels* were composed by Jean-Baptiste Moreau, who wrote the music for Racine's stage works for the convent school. Nevertheless, despite the clear connections between Racine, Moreau, and Saint-Cyr, the first musical settings of Racine's poems were not composed for the girls and ladies residing there. Instead, it is clear from contemporary accounts that Moreau's settings of what would later be published as Racine's first and third *Cantiques spirituels* (*Les méchants m'ont vanté* and *Mon Dieu, quelle guerre cruelle!*) first served as court entertainment of a devotional nature. The marquis de Dangeau reports their performance in the king's rooms at Fontainebleau on Saturday, 2 October 1694: "After dining, the king listened in his chamber to paraphrases by Racine of some chapters from Saint Paul. Moreau wrote the music."[3] Settings of Racine's other two poems soon followed, one by Moreau (*Quel charme vainqueur du monde*) and one by Lalande (*Heureux qui, de la sagesse*). The texts of all four *Cantiques spirituels* were published together in 1695 by Denys Thierry as *Cantiques spirituels faits par Monsieur R. . . . pour estre mis en musique*, and the musical settings by Moreau and Lalande were published by Christophe Ballard later that same year.

The order of poems in Ballard's collection is not the same as that used in Thierry's publication, nor is it the order in which they were written, leading to some confusion.[4] Also problematic is the fact that the musical forces indicated for the cantiques in the Ballard publication are not the same as those used in their performances before the king. As published, the first three cantiques by Moreau call only for solo dessus, a unison chorus of dessus voices, and basse continue. Moreau's preface "Au lecteur" notes, "If the curious wish to have all the parts and the symphonies, they must address themselves to M. Moreau."[5] The published edition thus seems to represent a reduced version, although it is impossible to tell how extensive Moreau's changes actually were. Nevertheless, the wording of the title page seems to suggest that the changes may not have extended far beyond the removal of the instrumental parts; on the title page, the pieces are referred to as "suitable for nuns" (*propres pour les dames religieuses*), while the introduction "Au lecteur" states specifically that "they have been composed to be sung with ease in religious houses."[6] On the other hand, three exemplars of the 1695 publication held in the Bibliothèque nationale offer versions of four alternative stanzas for two of Moreau's settings, although it is not clear whether they were written by Moreau or by a later composer.[7] Copied by hand at the end of each volume are duo and trio versions of the following stanzas: from *Les méchants m'ont vanté*, "Que je vois de Vertus" (for dessus and basse-taille voices) and "L'Amour sur tous les dons" (for two dessus voices and basse); and from *Mon Dieu, quelle guerre cruelle!*, "L'un tout esprit, et tout céleste" (for dessus and basse-taille) and "Ô grâce, ô rayon salutaire" (for dessus and basse). Interestingly, the published score includes alternative duo settings for three passages in Lalande's setting—the half-stanzas "Leur sainte et pénible vie" and "Dans une route insensée" and the stanza "De nos attentats injustes," all for two dessus voices—suggesting that a precedent for such alternative settings did indeed exist.[8] In any case, it is impossible to know for sure what forces originally performed Moreau's cantiques; the little we know about their performance at court is of no help, since the only performer mentioned was Moreau himself as singer.[9]

Also published in 1695 were Pascal Collasse's settings of Racine's *Cantiques spirituels*, which the composer dedicated to Madame de Maintenon: *Cantiques spirituels, mis en musique par P. Collasse, maistre de musique de la Chapelle du Roy* (Paris: Christophe Ballard, 1695). Collasse seems to have known of the settings by Moreau and Lalande, and perhaps others, for he notes in his dedication that "there is hardly a composer of any renown who has not thought he should exercise his genius upon these words that serve as the subject of the Airs that I have the honor to present to you."[10] Collasse makes use of larger musical forces than Moreau or Lalande; the setting calls not only for three solo dessus voices and a chorus of three dessus parts, but also instruments: two transverse flutes and two violins, accompanied by basse continue. The instruments are used for the short symphonies that precede each cantique and for instrumental ritournelles within the first, second, and fourth cantiques. These works are more complicated in their structure than the settings by Moreau and Lalande, with more textural and formal variety within each piece; this is discussed in more detail below. Although Collasse was best known for his work in opera, and (unlike Moreau) had no official relationship with Saint-Cyr, a connection to that convent school—or at least to its founder—would seem likely, given Collasse's dedication of the work to Madame de Maintenon and the presence of the publication in the holdings of the institution.[11]

Another composer to set Racine's four *Cantiques spirituels* was Jean-Noël Marchand, whose settings date from sometime before 1710.[12] Quite different in their approach from the settings of Moreau, Lalande, and Collasse, Marchand's works make use of large performing forces: solo singers (dessus, haute-contre, and basse), a three-part chorus (also consisting of dessus, haute-contre, and basse), and flutes and strings in various combinations. Marchand's melodic style is borrowed from French operatic traditions, and his structural approach recalls the *grand motet*. Each of his cantiques begins with a lengthy symphonie, the first of which reflects the style of a French overture: the first of its two sections is in a stately duple meter with marked dotted rhythms, and the second is in a livelier triple meter. In addition, instrumental ritournelles are often inserted between stanzas, and the instruments are used to accompany solo vocal and chorus sections. Such grand settings of *cantiques spirituels* were not typical, and Marchand's are among only a few that are known.[13]

Two other publications include smaller-scale musical settings of individual cantiques by Racine. Ballard's 1695 publication titled *Pseaumes et cantiques spirituels, mis en musique avec la basse-continue* includes settings of the second and third cantiques, *Heureux qui, de la sagesse* and *Mon Dieu, quelle guerre cruelle!* The collection was published anonymously but has been attributed to the obscure composer Duhalle. Another collection published by Ballard, *Airs spirituels des meilleurs autheurs* (1701), includes a setting by Jean-Baptiste de Bousset of the third stanza of Racine's third cantique.

The *Cantique spirituel* Tradition

In its simplest form, the *cantique spirituel* is a musical setting of a religious text in French to a melody either borrowed or newly composed. The genre traces its roots to the Geneva Psalter and the devotional music of the French Protestants, founded on verse translations of the psalms by Clément Marot and Théodore de Bèze. The powerful attraction of vernacular psalms was co-opted by the Counter-Reformation in its efforts to hamper the spread of Protestantism and to bring those who had strayed back into the Catholic fold. Other French texts were adopted for use in teaching religious doctrine and in private prayer; these included translations or paraphrases of Latin texts from the liturgy, as well original pious poetry, often strophic.[14] Musical settings of devotional poetry in French were at this time grouped together under general name of *cantiques spirituels* or *airs spirituels*.[15] The *cantiques spirituels* used in Counter-Reformation efforts typically were simple, regularly metered, and easy to memorize—suitable for indoctrinating children and the unlettered into the catechism.

Spiritual songs in French also played an important role in the struggle against *libertinage*, which thrived in the milieu of the salons frequented by courtiers. Salon poets created satirical and often licentious texts that were set to music by fashionable composers in the forms of the *air sérieux* or *air à boire*. According to Denise Launay, "The widow Ballard published them for the delectation of a public permeated by a philosophy of existence that mixed taunting with melancholy, tolerance with insolence, and which opposed the brevity of life with its renewed thirst for unceasing pleasures."[16] Learned, ornate *cantiques spirituels* deployed in the struggle against *libertinage* made frequent use of the practice of parody; authors and publishers took advantage of the ease with which words are recalled when sung to a melody by attaching their spiritual verses to well-known tunes. Many such collections appeared, often published anonymously, from *L'Amphion sacré* in 1615 to the *Opuscules sacrés et lyriques* of 1772.

A smaller part of this trend featured learned, ornate musical settings of high artistic quality; scholar Thierry Favier calls these *cantiques savants*, or "erudite" cantiques.[17] This type of cantique is seen in compositions by Étienne Moulinié and Henry Du Mont. Moulinié's *Meslanges de sujets chrestiens, cantiques, litanies, et motets*—published in 1658, but already completed by 1650[18]—sets texts taken from the *Paraphrase des pseaumes* (1648) and *Œuvres chrestiennes* (1633) of Antoine Godeau, Bishop of Grasse and Vence. In the *Meslanges*, Moulinié blends the lyric court style of solo singing with sections for chorus based on learned counterpoint. Du Mont also set texts by Godeau in his *Airs à quatre parties, avec la basse continue* (1663). The preface of this collection makes no allusion to pedagogy, missions, edification, or amusement, suggesting that Du Mont intended his settings purely as artistic creations.[19]

Rooted even more strongly in the stylistic tradition of the secular air are the *airs spirituels* of Bénigne de Bacilly, the first book of which appeared in 1672. When the first book was republished sometime between 1672 and 1677, most of the airs were given ornamented *doubles*, which brought the *air spirituel* into the realm of virtuosity. Bacilly's airs take on the form and style of the secular air; most are in the traditional small-scale binary form with repeats, and most involve similar practices of ornamentation. According to his preface, Bacilly composed his airs for teaching singing to young girls, particularly in convent schools, for whom the texts of worldly *airs sérieux* would have been inappropriate.

Even though Racine's poems and their settings belong within established traditions of religious poetry and *cantiques spirituels*, both music and text reflect competing stylistic trends within those traditions. On one hand, Racine's texts descend from strong traditions of biblical paraphrases, in which the meaning of the original text was paramount. At the same time, the poems are rooted firmly in a tradition of original religious verse. They are reflections on biblical passages but are not meant to be translations of them. The first cantique, *Les méchants m'ont vanté*, is "drawn" (*tiré*) from the thirteenth chapter of St. Paul's First Epistle to the Corinthians; the second, *Heureux qui, de la sagesse*, is based loosely on the fifth chapter of the book of Wisdom; and the third, *Mon Dieu, quelle guerre cruelle!*, paraphrases Romans 7:15–24. The final cantique, *Quel charme vainqueur du monde*, claims to be based on various passages (*divers endroits*) from Isaiah and Jeremiah, but it is actually a composite of several biblical verses and images.

On the whole, musical settings of Racine's *Cantiques spirituels* favor the trend of sophisticated, ornate music resembling the court airs pioneered by Bacilly. This is particularly true of the settings by Moreau, Duhalle, and Bousset. All are written for solo voice with basse continue accompaniment, and are similar in form to the secular air; each stanza is composed in two sections, with the first or both repeated. Lalande's setting of Racine's second cantique (placed fourth and last in Ballard's 1695 publication) generally follows this form as well, though it is set for one and two solo voices. The works by Collasse and Marchand employ more elaborate musical forces and structures, often relying on through-composed forms. Both include vocal solos, duos, and trios, as well as a three-part chorus, and make extensive use of instruments, with symphonies and ritournelles introducing major sections. Overall, both the poetic and musical aspects of all these works favor the artistic impulse over the didactic, and they fit well within the more sedate court atmosphere at the end of the seventeenth century, as Louis XIV turned from secular pleasures to more spiritual pursuits.

The Composers

Jean-Baptiste Moreau was born in Angers, probably in 1656, and died in Paris on 24 August 1733. His first royal commission was the divertissement *Les bergers de Marly*, in March 1688, a little more than a year after Madame de Maintenon and Louis XIV established the Maison royale de Saint-Louis at Saint-Cyr. Madame de Maintenon soon commissioned Moreau to compose music for Racine's play *Esther*, which the poet wrote for the girls of the royal school.[20] The success of the play, performed in January and February 1689, led to the commission of *Athalie* (1691), another collaboration between the poet and the composer. Moreau was reported to have been unstable professionally and in his social life, and he eventually became distanced from the Maison royale.[21] According to Edith Borroff and Anne Piéjus, Moreau's fall from favor was probably the result of his own bad conduct and his friendship with poet Alexandre Laînez, some of whose poems portray musicians as pleasure-seekers and heavy drinkers.[22] In November 1692, Moreau was appointed the *surintendant* of music for Languedoc, but he was back at court by 1694, when he was asked to set Racine's *Cantiques spirituels* to music. Moreau served briefly as *maître de musique* at Béziers Cathedral from December 1704 to sometime in 1705. No trace of him can be found after 1706.

Michel-Richard de Lalande was the most prominent of the composers who set Racine's *Cantiques spirituels*. Born in Paris on 15 December 1657, he died at Versailles on 18 June 1726. He received his training in the choir of the royal church of Saint Germain-l'Auxerrois in Paris and was invited at age twenty-two to contribute some *Leçons de Ténèbres* to the Holy Week repertory of the Sainte-Chapelle. Lalande served as the organist for four important Parisian churches and taught harpsichord to the daughter of the maréchal de Noailles, who recommended him to Louis XIV as a teacher for the king's daughters by Madame de Montespan. In 1683, on the retirement of Henry Du Mont and Pierre Robert from the royal chapel, Louis XIV held a competition to replace them with four musicians who would take turns fulfilling the duties on a quarterly basis. According to Alexandre Tannevot's "Discours sur la vie et les ouvrages de M. De la Lande" (1729), the king intervened in the process to secure a position for Lalande.[23] Lalande continued to acquire important royal positions, becoming one of the *compositeurs de la musique de la chambre* in 1685. In 1689, Lalande was appointed *surintendant de la musique de la chambre*, the most coveted musical position at court, and the king ordered the court copyists to make a complete manuscript of Lalande's *grands motets*. Although Lalande did not quite have the supreme control over music wielded by Lully, he acquired almost all of the royal posts available to him. By all accounts, he was well liked by the king, who is said to have remarked to him, after the deaths of the dauphin and Lalande's two daughters: "You have lost two daughters who were deserving of merit. I have lost Monseigneur.... La Lande, we must submit."[24] Lalande was primarily known for his *grands motets*; the single setting of Racine's text is one of his few sacred works for only one or two voices.[25]

Pascal Collasse was born in Reims in January 1649 and died at Versailles on 17 July 1709. In 1666, he succeeded Jean-François Lalouette as Lully's secretary and as *batteur de mesure* at the Paris Opéra, where he worked closely with the master. An important part of his job was composing inner vocal and instrumental parts after Lully had supplied the melody and bass. Collasse acknowledged his debt to Lully in prefaces to some of his works, but he was nevertheless accused of plagiarism and sued by Lully's family after Lully's death. In 1683, Collasse competed for one of the four positions as *sous-maître* for the royal chapel; no doubt Lully's support aided in his success at obtaining the position. Despite his work in the royal chapel, Collasse continued his association with the Académie royale as a composer of operas. Even though his musical roots were in traditional Lullian opera, Collasse is recognized as one of the least conservative composers of his generation, helping to establish the new genre of *opéra-ballet* with his *Ballet des saisons* (1695).[26] No details are known about the genesis of his settings of Racine's *Cantiques spirituels*. Although his collection *Cantiques spirituels, mis en musique* is dedicated to Madame de Maintenon and appeared shortly after the settings by Moreau and Lalande, we know of no direct connections to Racine, nor of any commission.

Jean-Baptiste de Bousset was known in his time as the leading composer of *airs sérieux et à boire*. He was born near Dijon in 1662 and died in Paris in 1725. After arriving in Paris in the early 1690s, Bousset held positions as *maître de musique* to the Académie française, the Académie des sciences, and the Académie des inscriptions, for which he composed and conducted motets for the feast day of St. Louis. According to L. E. S. J. Laborde, "His manner of singing was so delightful that he made a large fortune in Paris, singing airs which no one composed better than he did."[27] Bousset wrote 875 *airs sérieux et à boire*, bringing out a new book of airs each year for thirty-four years.[28] In *Le Parnasse françois*, Évrard Titon du Tillet wrote: "One finds in Bousset's airs an exact expression of the words; a noble, enjoyable, and natural melody; and, surprisingly, great variety among the large number of airs he composed."[29]

Little to nothing is known about the last two composers represented in this volume. Jean-Noël Marchand was baptized in Paris on 14 August 1666 and died there on 31 May 1710. He succeeded his father, Jean Marchand, as *ordinaire de la musique de la chambre* at age nine and entered the royal chapel in 1686 as an instrumentalist.[30] In 1698, he became the organist at Notre Dame de Versailles, and one month before his death, he was appointed lutenist to the royal chamber. Nothing at all is known about the composer Duhalle.

The Music

All of the musical settings of Racine's *Cantiques spirituels* reflect stylistic and formal characteristics of court airs and show a close kinship with Bacilly's *Airs spirituels*, the first works to apply the sophisticated musical style of the secular air to religious poetry in French. The settings differ primarily in the complexity of their musical forces and structure. All generally rely on a small-scale binary form of two repeated sections, a structure commonly seen in secular songs by Michel Lambert, Sébastien Le Camus, and other composers of *airs sérieux*. The cantiques by Duhalle and Bousset adhere more strictly to this form than do the settings by Moreau, Lalande, Collasse, and Marchand, in which often only the first half of each stanza is repeated. Sometimes the binary structure is dispensed with entirely, especially in the settings by Collasse and Marchand.

The relationship to the air can also be seen in the works' melodic character, which tends toward stepwise motion but uses wider leaps to create emotional tension and melodic distinctiveness. The settings are mostly syllabic, with occasional melismatic flourishes on important or evocative words. Melodies tend to avoid sequences and Italianate figuration, reflecting the clear influence of the Lullian operatic style on the secular air.

In addition, the sectional nature of the settings by Moreau, Lalande, Collasse, and especially Marchand recall the formal characteristics of the *grand motet*. These larger settings typically rely on the organization of Racine's poems for their structure. Individual stanzas are used as the basis for internal sections, which are delineated by changes in forces and texture, or by cadences, and are often variations of the small binary form. These works are not the first settings of religious texts in French to employ the form and style of *grands motets*: Claude Oudot's 1692 settings of verses from Abbé Testu's *Stances chrestiennes* also involve large forces and a variety of internal structures, including instrumental sections with labels like "Ouverture," "Gigue," "Gavotte," "Air," "Prelude," and "Chaconne."

The three settings by Moreau are of the first, third, and fourth poems printed in Denys Thierry's literary edition of Racine's *Cantiques spirituels*. As noted above, these works seem originally to have been composed with instrumental parts, none of which has survived. Nevertheless, the textures of the published music suggest that the instruments were unlikely to have been used to accompany the vocal part, since the settings are complete without any added instruments.[31] A more likely role for instruments would have been in ritournelles between vocal sections—possibly between stanzas, but mainly as opening symphonies to individual cantiques—indeed, symphonies (in the plural) are specifically mentioned in the note "Au lecteur."[32]

Textural variety in Moreau's settings is introduced through the alternation of solo voices and choir, and by changes in the range of the accompanying bass. Sometimes the basse continue part is written following the practice of *violons en basse*, in which the "bass" of the texture occupies a much higher range than normal, indicated by a C1 or treble clef. Not merely used for simple contrast, *violons en basse* technique plays a role in the musical rhetoric;[33] for example, the practice is found in stanza 11 of Moreau's first setting (*Les méchants m'ont vanté*, mm. 151–71), where words like *clartés*, *éclairera*, *cieux*, and *soleil* evoke images of brightness and heavenly light. In the next stanza, the basse continue returns to its normal range, highlighting the phrase "La Foi vive est le fondement."

The general structure of Moreau's settings closely follows that of Racine's poetry. Each stanza is given its own self-contained, harmonically closed section, with the stanzas set alternately for solo treble voice and a unison treble choir. The stanzas feature two basic musical structures: through-composed melodies whose phrases follow the grammar of the poetic stanza, and small binary forms, in which the stanza is divided in two, with either the first half or both halves repeated. Another aspect of Moreau's use of form is its relationship to what the composer refers to in his introduction "Au lecteur" as the "rule of cantiques": "Since they have been composed to be sung with ease in religious houses, they observe the rule of cantiques, which is to set several stanzas on a single melody for solo voice with basse continue."[34] Clearly Moreau is referring to the strophic nature of the simple *cantiques spirituels* that were popular at his time. Strictly speaking, Moreau's settings do not feature a single, fixed melody, sung to different stanzas of music, but a number of the stanzas feature recurring melodic outlines (in *Les méchants m'ont vanté*, for example, compare mm. 1–18 with mm. 57–68, and mm. 19–30 with mm. 31–42). In general, Moreau's first and second settings each feature two distinct melodies that are varied and decorated to form the basis of the different stanzas.

Lalande's setting of Racine's second cantique conforms quite well to Moreau's settings in terms of style and structure, but with important differences that make this piece stand out within the collection. The primary difference is in the musical forces used and in the resulting differences in texture: rather than contrasting a solo voice with a unison chorus, Lalande calls for only two solo voices, often used as a duo.[35] No basse continue part is provided in the first stanza, though this does not make *a cappella* performance the only possibility; the continuo could double the lower part, resulting in a *violons en basse* texture. Lalande includes optional settings for the third and fourth stanzas, which can be used to replace the repeat of the second half of the binary structure of each section. Additionally, for the fifth stanza, Lalande offers a choice between a complete solo setting and a complete duo setting. (The alternative versions of these stanzas are provided in the appendix to this edition.) Despite the differences in texture, Lalande adheres to the same musical structures as Moreau: each stanza is a self-contained musical section, and all stanzas but the first are binary in form, with each half repeated. (Lalande's first stanza is through-composed, with the melody and words first presented by the lower voice, then answered by the duo.)

Collasse's settings of Racine's four poems are grander and more complex than the works by Moreau and Lalande, featuring larger forces and greater freedom in both textures and formal structures. This greater structural freedom distances Collasse's works stylistically from the secular air and the *air spirituel* introduced by Bacilly. Collasse calls for pairs of violins and transverse flutes (*flûtes allemandes*) and for vocal forces consisting of solos, duos, and trios of dessus voices, as well as a three-part treble chorus. The instruments are used primarily in instrumental symphonies that divide the individual settings into discrete sections. The setting of Racine's first cantique, *Les méchants m'ont vanté*, is the longest, containing five symphonies to introduce its five major divisions.

The third cantique, *Mon Dieu, quelle guerre cruelle!*, is the shortest, introduced by only a single symphonie. The instruments are sometimes used to double the treble chorus and occasionally serve as obbligato instrumental accompaniment, particularly in the fourth cantique, *Quel charme vainqueur du monde*.

The stanzas of Collasse's cantiques are primarily through-composed, with relatively few binary structures and repeated sections. Even within this greater formal variety, however, Collasse pays careful attention to the structure of the poems; stanzas are treated as individual sections within each setting, differentiated primarily by changes of forces or of meter. Nevertheless, one stanza sometimes follows another directly, without any change in texture or forces: this is the case with the first two stanzas of the third cantique (*Mon Dieu, quelle guerre cruelle!*, mm. 34–70). Collasse's settings most often feature a solo dessus voice accompanied by basse continue, but they also include a variety of duos, trios, and three-part choruses, often repeating the text or musical phrase first presented by solo voices; in *Les méchants m'ont vanté*, for example, the first half of the fourth stanza is first presented by a trio of solo voices (mm. 127–33), then echoed by the chorus (mm. 133–39), which then goes on to complete the stanza (mm. 140–45). The last section of each setting shows the greatest variety in instrumentation, texture, and structure; the grandest finale is reserved for the last of the cantiques (*Quel charme vainqueur du monde*, mm. 251–335), which features alternations of solos and chorus, both with and without instruments.

As presented in their original publication, Collasse's cantiques would seem to be beyond the capabilities of most convents of nuns, since they are on a much larger scale than the simpler, air-like settings by Moreau, Lalande, Bousset, and Duhalle. Yet Collasse, in his introduction "Au lecteur," reassures would-be performers of the ease of his works, and he lists a number of possible adaptations to make them suitable for all kinds of performing forces. These will be discussed below in the "Notes on Performance."

Marchand's settings of Racine's *Cantiques spirituels* are even more elaborate than Collasse's in their musical forces and structure. Like Collasse, Marchand includes instrumental parts other than basse continue, but they are used in a greater variety of combinations than in Collasse's settings. The first cantique (*Les méchants m'ont vanté*) includes pairs of violins and flutes, but the third (*Mon Dieu, quelle guerre cruelle!*) calls only for a pair of violins, and the other two settings require four string parts in addition to the basse continue.[36] With the exception of *Mon Dieu, quelle guerre cruelle!*, which is set for a solo bass voice, all of Marchand's cantiques feature three voice parts—dessus, haute-contre, and basse—that appear in various combinations throughout the collection.

Marchand's cantiques are primarily through-composed, although some stanzas are in binary form, with one or both halves repeated. The overall musical structure principally follows the poetic structure of the texts; stanzas are typically differentiated by strong cadences or a change of forces or meter, and they are often separated by instrumental passages. This is especially clear in the second cantique (*Heureux qui, de la sagesse*), in which each stanza is introduced by an instrumental passage, some labeled "Symphonie." In three places, instrumental ritournelles occur in the middle of stanzas: in the fourth stanza of *Mon Dieu, quelle guerre cruelle!* (mm. 95–101) and in the first and sixth stanzas of *Quel charme vainqueur du monde* (mm. 21–31 and 217–22). The great variety in forces, structure, texture, and melodic style make Marchand's pieces the grandest and most elaborate settings of Racine's poems, giving them something of the character of the *grand motet;* they are among the few settings of French devotional poetry in this style.

The pieces by Duhalle and Bousset are on a much smaller scale than the works just discussed. Their settings are of individual cantiques (or parts thereof) for solo dessus voice with basse continue accompaniment. Duhalle's settings of Racine's second and third cantiques are included within his collection *Pseaumes et cantiques spirituels,* published by Christophe Ballard in 1695. Each setting is divided into "versets" corresponding to the stanzas of the poem; all feature the same forces and structure. Each verset is composed as a self-contained section, beginning with a short prelude for the basse continue and continuing in a small binary form with each half repeated. These preludes range from four to thirteen measures long and are not included in the repeat of the first half of the melody. Bousset's "Hélas! en guerre avec moi-même" takes its text from the third stanza of Racine's third poem, and it is set in a simple binary form with each half repeated; unlike the settings by Duhalle, it includes no prelude for basse continue, and its melody is composed over a repeated four-measure bass pattern. It stands out from the other settings for its simplicity.

Notes on Performance

Because of their simplicity and small scope, the cantiques by Bousset and Duhalle offer no particular problems in performance beyond the choice of continuo instruments and the role of ornamentation. Since these works were originally intended as chamber music, harpsichord or archlute would be most appropriate on the basse continue parts, though chamber organ would also be suitable. A cello or viola da gamba may join the bass line, though it would also be possible to perform the works without a bowed bass instrument. The reprises in the binary forms offer an opportunity for ornamentation, a practice common in the secular air. Bacilly's treatise on singing, *Remarques curieuses sur l'art de bien chanter* (1668), provides a detailed discussion of the ornamentation of airs, with examples. In addition, a direct example of ornamentation is found in Collasse's setting of Racine's first cantique, which includes an engraved *double* for the fifth stanza, "Oui, mon Dieu, quand mes mains" (mm. 192–211). This section provides an appropriate model for the ornamentation of reprises in the other works in this volume.

Two sentences in the foreword "Au lecteur" of the original publication of the *Cantiques spirituels* by Moreau and Lalande suggest a number of possibilities for performance: "The airs are all independent. Some are suitable for dessus voices, others for bass or bas-dessus voices."[37] The first sentence could simply mean that each of the four cantiques can be performed on its own as an independent setting, but it may also mean that individual stanzas within a single cantique could be extracted for performance; each stanza concludes with a double bar, is harmonically closed, and is similar in length and structure to contemporary airs (including Bousset's and Duhalle's settings of Racine's individual stanzas). In any case, modern performers could certainly perform any of the four cantiques individually, or program all four, or group the three pieces by Moreau as a set, without the one by Lalande. Presenting Moreau's settings alone would standardize the performing ensemble and allow the performance to conclude with the larger forces of the unison choir.

Moreau also indicates that voice types other than dessus are appropriate, mentioning specifically bass and bas-dessus. However, specific voices are not identified by clef in the print; the treble clef (G2) is used almost exclusively in the vocal parts, with a few occurrences of soprano clef (C1). Because the range is generally consistent throughout (from d' to an occasional g"), a bas-dessus voice should be able to sing all the verses, perhaps with the exception of some that maintain a higher tessitura, such as "Un jour Dieu cessera" and "Nos clartés ici-bas" in *Les méchants m'ont vanté*. Unfortunately, Moreau does not specify which musical sections he considers suitable for male bass voices; sections that feature bass lines in a high register (the *violons en basse* texture) can be ruled out, because the melodies would have to be sung down an octave and would thus lie below the bass line.

One could also omit the unison choir and perform Moreau's cantiques with a soloist or a group of soloists. Moreau makes no mention of the choir in his introduction, and there is no great musical difference between the *seul* and *chœur* sections. One of Moreau's indications regarding the use of the choir is ambiguous; the last verse of *Quel charme vainqueur du monde* bears the heading "Seule, et Chœur en suite" (m. 133), with no subsequent clarification of when the choir should enter. The most logical point is at the second statement of the text "Chacun peut boire en cette onde" (mm. 145–47), which also repeats the music of the first statement (mm. 141–43).

In the works by Moreau, Collasse, and Marchand, several sections feature *violons en basse,* which raises a number of questions on basse continue instrumentation. In most of these sections, the basse continue part simply changes clef from F4 to C1 or C3, with no indication given as to which string part—if any—might double the high "bass." If the basse continue is played on a cello or viola da gamba in a modern-day performance, the instrument could continue playing in the high passage if it is capable of reaching all the pitches included; if not, it should drop out for the entire passage. In works involving violins, one or more violins may play the high bass line. In any case, the keyboard instrument may continue playing the bass line at the pitches indicated, adding chords in the right hand within the limited range available to it.

An exception to the above is found in Collasse's setting of *Quel charme vainqueur du monde*, where, in three passages, the score indicates a change in the instrument that plays the basse continue (mm. 32–59, mm. 85–113, and mm. 251–80). In the first of these sections, the line for the basse continue part is omitted, and the second violin line is placed below the voice, with the indication "Second violon seul," but no figures. With the first violin line placed above the voice, the intention here seems to be a trio of two solo violins and voice. The lines are arranged similarly in the other two of these *violons en basse* sections, but the indications are different. In measures 85–113, the voice is accompanied by two solo flutes and a part labeled "Violon," which could refer to either of the violin parts, or to both playing together. In measure 95, this same line is given a different indication midphrase: "B.C. Violon." This cue may have been provided to correct or clarify the indication given in measure 85, and it probably represents no change in intention. I have assigned the violin line in this passage to the second violin, but it could be played by either violin, or by both; in any case, it is clearly meant to serve as the basse continue, even though no figures are provided. This does not necessarily rule out the use of the keyboard, since the original score in general is not completely figured; the choice can be left up to performers. Similarly, at measure 251, the bottom line of the original score is labeled "B.C. 2. Violon," indicating that a violin is intended to serve as the basse continue voice through the end of the section (m. 280). Again, no figures are given, but the keyboard player may play along on the part if desired.

Collasse's setting provides a large number of performance options, outlined in his introduction "Au lecteur":

> It should be noted that these cantiques were composed very simply in the pure explication of the words. All of them can be sung by a solo voice, since the melody always prevails in the highest voice.
> If there are two [singers] together, they can make a pleasant ensemble by singing the second or the third dessus [with the top voice]. If there are three, the concert will be more perfect.
> Although there only seem to be dessus in this work, nevertheless all kinds of persons can sing it with equal voices. But when instruments are included, the basse continue should be played an octave lower if the cantiques are sung by tailles....
> Thus this work is very easy to perform, because it has been written in such a way that one always finds there a simple and agreeable harmony, even with as few instruments as you wish.[38]

Collasse's first option is to perform the work with a single dessus voice and continuo, without the other voices or choir. This would seem to be less than desirable, however. In a number of places in the score, musical passages sung by a solo or group of soloists are repeated by choir; the antiphonal effect would be lost in a performance by solo voice. Moreover, solo performance would eliminate much of the contrast provided by differing numbers of solo voices. Like Moreau, Collasse suggests that voice types other than dessus can sing his cantiques. But Collasse also makes use of *violons en basse*, most notably at the end of each setting. In passages sung by a solo tenor (taille), the basse continue would have to be performed down an octave—an arrangement that seems acceptable to Collasse, but one that might rob those passages of their special character.

Collasse also indicates that his settings can be performed without instruments, or with as few as the performers wish. But because a few sections feature obbligato instruments, what is possible may not be what is most desirable. One could certainly reduce the instruments in the first and third movements to either a pair of violins or flutes, since the parts most often simply double each other. Omitting the string parts from *Heureux qui, de la sagesse* and *Quel charme vainqueur du monde* would be more problematic, since they play lengthy introductions to vocal sections and interludes within them. Even though Collasse may have composed the vocal parts so that they make a "simple and agreeable harmony" on their own, the string parts would be sorely missed if omitted.

The manuscript source of Marchand's cantiques suffers from an unfortunate lack of precision in performance intentions. Most glaringly, there are no indications of whether the sections for three vocal parts are intended to be sung by soloists or choir. The only exception is in the final stanza of *Quel charme vainqueur du monde*, where we find "Chœur" written above the vocal parts (m. 209). This section immediately follows one for three voices alone, with no basse continue or obbligato instruments (mm. 200–208); the music of the section for chorus repeats exactly what was presented by the three voices alone, but with the full complement of obbligato strings and basse continue. Clearly measures 200–208 are intended for solo voices, which are then echoed by the full vocal and instrumental ensemble. By extension, it is possible to argue that the other three-voice passages in this cantique are intended for three soloists, and this has been indicated at the appropriate points in the edition. Nevertheless, one could certainly perform these sections chorally if desired.

Marchand's indications for instruments are relatively clear. Parts for flutes, strings, and "tous" (tutti) are clearly labeled in *Les méchants m'ont vanté*, and string parts are labeled consistently in the other three cantiques. Though all the upper string parts are labeled simply "violon," the cleffing of the parts in the source implies the use of specific violin sizes (*dessus de violon, haute-contre de violon*, etc.). In this edition, the three highest string parts in *Heureux qui, de la sagesse* and *Quel charme vainqueur du monde*, which are notated in G1 and C1 clefs in the original, are assigned to violins, while the fourth part, originally notated in C2, is assigned to viola. In general, the basse continue part would be played by cello or viola da gamba, and it could even be doubled by contrabass in an especially full texture. Moreover, violins can double the basse continue line in *violons en basse* passages. Given its numerous instrumental ritournelles and symphonies, Marchand's cantiques—unlike Collasse's—cannot be performed without instruments.

Notes

1. Thierry Favier, "Les cantiques spirituels de Racine mis en musique: Aspects esthétiques d'un succès programmé," *La Licorne* 50 (1999): 103.

2. Thierry Favier, *Le chant des muses chrétiennes: Cantique spirituel et dévotion en France (1685–1715)* (Paris: Société française de musicologie, 2008), 24.

3. "Le Roi, après dîner entendit dans sa chambre des paraphrases qu'a faites Racine sur quelques chapitres de saint Paul. Moreau a fait la musique." Marquis de Dangeau (Philippe de Courcillon), as quoted by Favier, *Chant des muses chrétiennes*, 26 n. 40. Translations are mine unless otherwise noted. Although Dangeau's memoir does not report it, Moreau was the first to perform his own cantiques. This is confirmed by a letter from Racine to the poet Nicolas Boileau of 28 September 1694: "Il [Moreau] est ici, et le Roi doit les lui entendre chanter au premier jour." *Œuvres de J. Racine*, ed. Paul Mesnard, vol. 7 (Paris: Hachette, 1870), 132–33. Further evidence that the composer was the first performer of these works is found in the "Epitre au lecteur" in Christophe Ballard's 1699 publication *Receuil d'airs spirituels, cantiques et noëls de différents auteurs*, which also included Moreau's cantiques: "Sa Majesté, que la Pieté accompagne jusques dans ses momens de recreation, s'est long-temps reservé ces Cantiques, et la voix de l'Autheur pour les luy chanter." Quoted in Favier, *Chant des muses chrétiennes*, 140.

4. The order of Racine's *Cantiques spirituels* as published by Thierry is presented in the "Texts and Translations." However, Racine is known to have written the third cantique before the second. In the collection of works by Moreau and Lalande, Lalande's setting of Racine's second cantique, *Heureux qui, de la sagesse*, is placed last. It is not known exactly when Lalande composed this setting, nor do we know the extent of his participation in the publication. It has been assumed that Moreau was the principal actor in the publication, since the introduction titled "Au lecteur" refers to instrumental parts that could be obtained at that composer's residence (see note 5). The impression is that Lalande's setting was included in the publication for the sake of completeness.

5. "Si quelques Curieux desirent les avoir avec toutes les Parties & les Symphonies, ils n'auront qu'à s'adresser à M. Moreau." Jean-Baptiste Moreau, "Au lecteur," *Cantiques chantez devant le Roy* (Paris: Christophe Ballard, 1695).

6. "Ils ont été faits pour être aisément chantez dans des Maisons Religieuses...". Moreau, "Au lecteur," *Cantiques chantez devant le Roy*. Thierry Favier regards the published version as a simplification of what was performed for the king at Versailles (Favier, "Cantiques spirituels de Racine mis en musique," 104). Because no manuscript survives of what was performed at Versailles, there is no way to prove or disprove this. I tend to think the published version is not necessarily a simplified version, since Moreau's "Au lecteur" states they were "composed" (*fait*) to be suitable for singing in religious houses.

7. Favier, *Chant des muses chrétiennes*, 313. These settings are included in the appendix.

8. These settings are included in the appendix.

9. See note 3 above.

10. "Il n'y a presque point de Compositeur un peu célebre, qui n'ait crû devoir exercer son genie sur les mesmes paroles qui servent de sujet aux Airs que j'ay l'honneur de vous presenter." Pascal Collasse, *Cantiques spirituels, mis en musique* (Paris: Christophe Ballard, 1695), [ii]. Included among these most celebrated composers is Michel Lambert, according to the poet Pierre Bellocq in a poem honoring Racine; unfortunately, Lambert's setting is lost (Favier, *Chant des muses chrétiennes*, 141).

11. Collasse's *Cantiques spirituels, mis en musique* is listed in inventories drawn up in 1790 and 1795, and copies of the publication with the *ex libris* of Saint-Cyr are found in the Bibliothèque nationale and in the Bibliothèque municipale de Versailles. See Marie Robert, "Inventaire des livres de musique de l'institut Saint-Louis de Saint-Cyr," *XVIIe siècle* 34 (1957): 93–105; and Favier, *Chant des muses chrétiennes*, 160–67.

12. A facsimile edition of the manuscript is available in Jean-Noël Marchand, *Cantiques spirituels*, ed. Thierry Favier (Courlay, France: Éditions J. M. Fuzeau, 1999).

13. Perhaps most notable of these is Claude Oudot's 1692 setting of the Abbé Testu's *Stances chrétiennes* (Paris: Denys Thierry, 1669).

14. Denise Launay, *La musique religieuse en France du Concile de Trente à 1804* (Paris: Société française de musicologie, 1993), 88–89.

15. Scholars have tended to reserve the term *airs spirituels* for musical settings with original melodies, with *cantiques spirituels* referring to settings with melodies borrowed, or parodied, from popular songs and airs. Cf. Favier, *Chant des muses chrétiennes*, esp. 45ff.

16. "La veuve Ballard les publie pour la délectation d'un public imprégné par cette philosophie de l'existence qui mêle le persiflage à la mélancolie, la tolérance à l'insolence et qui oppose à la brièveté de la vie sa soif de plaisirs sans cesse renouvelée." Launay, *Musique religieuse en France*, 180.

17. See Favier, *Chant des muses chrétiennes*.

18. Launay, *Musique religieuse en France*, 363.

19. Ibid., 370.

20. Because of Moreau's close involvement with *Esther*, some scholars have identified him as the *maître de musique* for Saint-Cyr. No evidence supports this assumption: no contracts survive, nor is there any other mention of Moreau as music master in contemporary memoirs of the institution. In fact, the *maître de musique* at Saint-Cyr was not Moreau but Guillaume-Gabriel Nivers; he composed and arranged almost all the music used at the beginning of the institution, particularly liturgical chant and motets.

21. *Grove Music Online* (hereafter *GMO*), Oxford Music Online (http://www.oxfordmusiconline.com), s.v. "Moreau, Jean-Baptiste," by Edith Borroff and Anne Piéjus.

22. *GMO*, "Moreau."

23. The "Discours" serves as the preface to the posthumous engraved edition (1729–34) of many of Lalande's works. *GMO*, s.v. " Lalande, Michel-Richard de," by James R. Anthony and Lionel Sawkins.

24. *GMO*, "Lalande."

25. Lalande composed one other *cantique spirituel* that survives: *Tandis que Babylone*, published in *Nouvelles poésies spirituelles et morales* (Paris, 1732). Lalande also composed a small number of *petits motets*, of which only eleven survive, as well as three surviving *Leçons de Ténèbres*.

26. *Die Musik in Geschichte und Gegenwart*, 2nd ed., *Personenteil*, s.v. "Collasse (Colasse), Pascal" (col. 1384), by Jérôme de La Gorce.

27. Leon Emmanuel Simon Joseph de Laborde, *Musiciens de Paris, 1536–1792*, as quoted in *GMO*, s.v. "Bousset, Jean-Baptiste (Drouard) de," by Greer Garden.

28. Évrard Titon du Tillet, *Le Parnasse françois* (1732; repr. Geneva: Slatkine Reprints, 1971), 604.

29. Titon du Tillet, *Parnasse françois*, 604: "On trouve dans la composition des Airs de Bousset une expression juste des paroles, un chant noble, agréable & naturel; &, ce qui est surprenant, une grande varieté dans le grand nombre qu'il en a donné."

30. *GMO*, s.v. "Marchand, Jean-Noël," by David Fuller and Bruce Gustafson.

31. As indicated in note 6 above, Thierry Favier regards the published version as a broad recomposition of the original. I am

more inclined to assume there would be few major differences between the two versions, if the original ever resurfaced.

32. See note 5 above.

33. See Deborah Kauffman, "*Violons en basse* as Musical Allegory," *Journal of Musicology* 23, no. 1 (2006): 153–85.

34. "Et comme ils ont été faits pour être aisément chantez dans des Maisons Religiuses, on y a observé la regle des Cantiques, qui est de faire passer plusieurs Stances sur une même modulation à voix seul avec la Basse-Continuë." Moreau, "Au lecteur," *Cantiques chantez devant le Roy*.

35. In contemporary usage, the term "duo" implied two solo voices; the term "chœur" is never used in Lalande's setting.

36. Although the string parts are labeled simply *violon*, they parallel the traditional five-part strings used in a French orchestra: *dessus de violon, haute-contre de violon, taille de violon, quinte de violon,* and *basse de violon* (on the basse continue part).

37. "Ce sont tous Airs détachez. Les uns sont propres aux voix de Dessus, les autres aux voix de Basses, ou de Bas-Dessus." Moreau, "Au lecteur," *Cantiques chantez devant le Roy*.

38. Collasse, "Au lecteur," *Cantiques spirituels, mis en musique*:

> On les peut chanter tous à Voix seule, parce que le Sujet regne toûjours dans la Partie la plus haute.
>
> Si l'on se trouve deux ensemble on peut faire un Concert agreable, en chantant le Second ou le Troisième Dessus. Si l'on est trois, le Concert sera plus parfait.
>
> Quoy qu'il ne paroisse que des Dessus dans cét Ouvrage, neanmoins toutes sortes de Personnes les peuvent chanter à Voix égales. Mais quand on y joindra les Instrumens, il faudra joüer la Basse-Continuë une Octave plus bas, lorsque les susdits Cantiques seront chantez par des Tailles....
>
> Ainsi cet Ouvrage est tres-aisé à executer, parce qu'il est fait de maniere à y trouver toûjours une Harmonie simple & agreable, mesme avec si peu d'Instruments que l'on voudra.

Texts and Translations

Throughout the edition, the spelling and punctuation of the cantique texts have been modernized and standardized to conform to the most recent edition of Jean Racine's *Cantiques spirituels* (*Cantiques spirituels et autres poèmes*, ed. Jean-Pierre Lemaire [Paris: Éditions Gallimard, 1999], 15–26). The poem texts are given here in the same order in which they appeared in their first literary publication (*Cantiques spirituels faits par Monsieur R. . . . pour estre mis en musique* [Paris: Denys Thierry, 1695]). Minor orthographical differences in the various musical sources are not noted, though a few settings contain more substantive textual changes; these are given both in endnotes below and in the critical notes to each musical setting (see the critical report). English translations are the work of the editor and strive to be as literal as possible, though in a few instances syntax and phrase order have been altered to make the meaning clear in English.

Les méchants m'ont vanté

Cantique premier : À la louange de la charité
Tiré de saint Paul : I Corinth, chap. 13

Les méchants m'ont vanté leurs mensonges frivoles ;
    Mais je n'aime que les paroles
    De l'éternelle Vérité.
    Plein du feu divin qui m'inspire,
    Je consacre aujourd'hui ma lyre
    À la céleste Charité.
En vain je parlerais le langage des anges ;
    En vain, mon Dieu, de tes louanges
    Je remplirais tout l'univers :
    Sans amour, ma gloire n'égale
    Que la gloire de la cymbale
    Qui d'un vain bruit frappe les airs.
Que sert à mon esprit de percer les abîmes
    Des mystères les plus sublimes,
    Et de lire dans l'avenir ?
    Sans amour, ma science est vaine
    Comme le songe dont à peine
    Il reste un léger souvenir.
Que me sert que ma foi transporte les montagnes,
    Que dans les arides campagnes
    Les torrents naissent sous mes pas,
    Ou que ranimant la poussière,
    Elle rende aux morts la lumière
    Si l'amour ne l'anime pas ?
Oui, mon Dieu, quand mes mains de tout mon héritage
    Aux pauvres feraient le partage ;
    Quand même pour le nom chrétien,
    Bravant les croix les plus infâmes,

First Cantique: In praise of Charity
Drawn from Saint Paul: I Corinthians, chapter 13

The wicked have flattered me with their frivolous lies;
    but I care only for the words
    of eternal Truth.
    Full of the divine fire that inspires me,
    today I dedicate my lyre
    to heavenly Charity.
In vain I would speak the language of the angels;
    in vain, my God, with your praises
    I would fill the entire universe.
    Without love, my glory equals
    only that of the cymbal
    that strikes the air with a vain noise.
What avails it my spirit to see into the abysmal depths
    of the most sublime mysteries
    and to read the future?
    Without love, my learning is unavailing,
    like the dream of which
    barely a scant memory remains.
What avails it me if my faith moves mountains,
    if in the arid countryside
    torrents spring from beneath my steps,
    or that, reviving the dust of the earth,
    my faith gives light to the dead,
    if love does not animate it?
Yes, my God, were my hands to share my entire
    inheritance among the poor—
    were I even, for the name of a Christian,
    braving the most infamous afflictions,

Je livrerais mon corps aux flammes,	to deliver my body to the flames—
Si je n'aime, je ne suis rien.	if I do not love, I am nothing.
Que je vois de Vertus qui brillent sur ta trace,	How many virtues I see lighting your path,
Charité, fille de la Grâce !	Charity, daughter of Grace!
Avec toi marche la Douceur,	With you walks Sweetness,
Que suit, avec un air affable,	and with an affable air,
La Patience inséparable	Patience follows, inseparable
De la Paix, son aimable sœur.	from Peace, her beloved sister.
Tel que l'astre du jour écarte les Ténèbres,	As the day star dispels Darkness,
De la Nuit compagnes funèbres,	funereal companion of Night,
Telle tu chasses d'un coup d'œil	so you chase away with a glance
L'envie aux humains si fatale,	Envy, so fatal to humans,
Et toute la troupe infernale	and all the infernal troop
Des Vices, enfants de l'orgueil.	of Vices, children of Pride.
Libre d'ambition, simple, et sans artifice,	Free from ambition, simple, and without artifice,
Autant que tu hais l'injustice,	as much as you hate Injustice,
Autant la vérité te plaît.	so much does Truth please you.
Que peut la colère farouche	What hold can fierce anger exert
Sur un cœur que jamais ne touche	on the heart that is never touched by
Le soin de son propre intérêt ?	concern for self-interest?
Aux faiblesses d'autrui loin d'être inexorable,	Far from being unforgiving toward our weaknesses,
Toujours d'un voile favorable	you instead always strive
Tu t'efforces de les couvrir.	to cover them with a favorable veil.
Quel triomphe manque à ta gloire ?	What need has your glory for a triumph?
L'Amour sait tout vaincre, tout croire,[1]	Love knows how to conquer all, to believe all,
Tout espérer, et tout souffrir.	to hope for everything, and to endure everything.
Un jour Dieu cessera d'inspirer des oracles ;	One day God will cease to inspire oracles;
Le don des langues, les miracles,	the gift of languages, miracles,
La science aura son déclin.	learning will have their decline.
L'Amour, la Charité divine,	Love, divine Charity,
Éternelle en son origine,	eternal in its origin,
Ne connaîtra jamais de fin.	will never know an end.
Nos clartés ici-bas ne sont qu'énigmes sombres ;	Our lights here below are only dark enigmas,
Mais Dieu, sans voiles et sans ombres,	but God, without veils and without shadows,
Nous éclairera dans les cieux ;	will light our way in the heavens,
Et ce Soleil inaccessible,	and this unapproachable Sun
Comme à ses yeux je suis visible,	will be made visible to my eyes,
Se rendra visible à mes yeux.	as I am visible to his eyes.
L'Amour sur tous les dons l'emporte avec justice.	Love justly outweighs all gifts.
De notre céleste édifice	Living Faith is the foundation
La Foi vive est le fondement ;	of our celestial edifice.
La sainte Espérance l'élève,	Holy Hope erects it,
L'ardente Charité l'achève	ardent Charity crowns it
Et l'assure éternellement.	and assures its existence for eternity.
Quand pourrai-je[2] t'offrir, ô Charité suprême,	When will I be able to offer you, O supreme Charity,
Au sein de la lumière même,	in the bosom of light itself,
Le cantique de mes[3] soupirs ;	the song of my sighs;
Et toujours brûlant pour ta gloire,	and burning for your glory always,
Toujours puiser, et toujours boire	forever draw, and forever drink
Dans la source des vrais plaisirs ?	from the spring of true pleasures?

Heureux qui, de la sagesse

  Cantique second : Sur le bonheur des
  justes et sur le malheur des réprouvés,
  tiré de la Sagesse, chap. 5

Heureux qui, de la sagesse
Attendant tout son secours,
N'a point mis en la richesse
L'espoir de ses derniers jours !

  Second Cantique: On the happiness of the
  just and the unhappiness of reprobates,
  drawn from Wisdom, chapter 5

Happy is he who, from wisdom
awaiting his final relief,
has not put the hope of his last days
in riches!

La mort n'a rien qui l'étonne ; Et dès que son Dieu l'ordonne, Son âme prenant l'essor S'élève d'un vol rapide Vers la demeure où réside Son véritable trésor.	Death has nothing to dismay him, and as soon as his God orders it, his soul, soaring up, rises in rapid flight toward the abode where his true treasure lies.
De quelle douleur profonde Seront un jour pénétrés Ces insensés qui du monde, Seigneur, vivent enivrés, Quand, par une fin soudaine Détrompés d'une ombre vaine Qui passe et ne revient plus, Leurs yeux du fond de l'abîme Près de ton trône sublime Verront briller tes élus !	What profound sorrow will one day penetrate these madmen who live intoxicated with the world, Lord, when at their sudden death, disabused of a vain shadow that passes and returns not, from the bottom of the abyss, their eyes will see your elect shining beside your sublime throne!
« Infortunés que nous sommes, Où s'égaraient nos esprits ? Voilà, diront-ils, ces hommes, Vils objets de nos mépris. Leur sainte et pénible vie Nous parut une folie ; Mais aujourd'hui triomphants, Le ciel chante leur louange Et Dieu lui-même les range Au nombre de ses enfants.	"Unfortunate ones that we are, where did our spirits go astray? There," they will say, "are those men, the vile objects of our contempt. Their holy and painful life seemed folly to us, but today, triumphant, the heavens sing their praise and God himself numbers them among his children.
« Pour trouver un bien fragile Qui nous vient d'être arraché, Par quel chemin difficile Hélas ! nous avons marché ! Dans une route insensée Notre âme en vain s'est lassée, Sans se reposer jamais, Fermant l'œil à la lumière Qui nous montrait la carrière De la bienheureuse paix.	"To find a fragile boon that will be wrested from us, alas, we have walked along such a difficult path! Along a senseless route our souls have grown weary in vain, without ever resting, closing our eyes to the light that showed us the path of blessed peace.
« De nos attentats injustes Quel fruit nous est-il resté ? Où sont les titres augustes Dont notre orgueil s'est flatté ? Sans amis et sans défense, Au trône de la vengeance Appelés en jugement, Faibles et tristes victimes, Nous y venons de nos crimes Accompagnés seulement. »	"What fruit remains of our ill-founded schemes? Where are the august titles that our pride preened itself on? Without friends and without defense, at the throne of retribution, called to judgment, weak and sad victims, we come accompanied only by our crimes."
Ainsi, d'une voix plaintive, Exprimera ses remords La pénitence tardive Des inconsolables morts. Ce qui faisait leurs délices, Seigneur, fera leurs supplices ; Et par une égale loi Tes saints trouveront des charmes Dans le souvenir des larmes Qu'ils versent ici pour toi.	Thus with a plaintive voice the tardy penitence of the inconsolable dead expresses its remorse. That which delighted them, Lord, will be their torment; and by an equable law your saints will find charms in the memory of the tears that they pour out for you now.

Mon Dieu, quelle guerre cruelle!

*Cantique troisième : Plainte d'un
Chrétien sur les contrariétés qu'il
éprouve au dedans de lui-même
Tiré de saint Paul : aux Romains, chap. 7*

Mon Dieu, quelle guerre cruelle !
Je trouve deux hommes en moi ;
L'un veut que plein d'amour pour toi
Mon cœur te soit toujours fidèle.
L'autre à tes volontés rebelle
Me révolte contre ta loi.

L'un tout esprit, et tout céleste,
Veut qu'au ciel sans cesse attaché,
Et des biens éternels touché,
Je compte pour rien tout le reste ;
Et l'autre par son poids funeste
Me tient vers la terre penché.

Hélas ! en guerre avec moi-même,
Où pourrai-je trouver la paix ?
Je veux, et n'accomplis jamais.
Je veux, mais, ô misère extrême !
Je ne fais pas le bien que j'aime,
Et je fais le mal que je hais.

Ô grâce, ô rayon salutaire,
Viens me mettre avec moi d'accord ;
Et domptant par un doux effort
Cet homme qui t'est si contraire,
Fais ton esclave volontaire
De cet esclave de la mort.

Quel charme vainqueur du monde

*Cantique quatrième : Sur les vaines
occupations des gens du siècle
Tiré de divers endroits d'Isaïe et de Jérémie*

Quel charme vainqueur du monde
Vers Dieu m'élève aujourd'hui ?
Malheureux l'homme qui fonde
Sur les hommes son appui !
Leur gloire fuit, et s'efface
En moins de temps que la trace
Du vaisseau qui fend les mers,
Ou de la flèche rapide
Qui loin de l'œil qui la guide
Cherche l'oiseau dans les airs.

De la Sagesse immortelle
La voix tonne, et nous instruit.
« Enfants des hommes, dit-elle,
De vos soins quel est le fruit ?
Par quelle erreur, âmes vaines,
Du plus pur sang de vos veines
Achetez-vous si souvent,
Non un pain qui vous repaisse,
Mais une ombre qui vous laisse
Plus affamés que devant ?

*Third Cantique: Lament of a
Christian on the contraries that
he experiences within himself
Drawn from Saint Paul: Epistle to the Romans, chapter 7*

My God, what cruel war!
I find two men within myself;
one, full of love for you,
wants my heart to be forever faithful to you.
The other, rebelling against your will,
turns me to revolt against your law.

One, all spirit and all celestial,
wants that, bound ceaselessly to the heavens
and touched by eternal good,
I should count all the rest as nothing;
and the other, by its fatal weight,
holds me, bent down, toward earth.

Alas, at war with myself,
where can I find peace?
I want, and never achieve.
I want, but—O extreme misery!—
I do not the good that I love,
and I do the evil that I hate.

O grace, O beneficial beam,
come reconcile me to myself;
and, taming with a gentle effort
this man who is so untrue to you,
make your willing slave
of this slave to death.

*Fourth Cantique: On the vain occu-
pations of the people of the world
Drawn from various parts of Isaiah and Jeremiah*

What charm victorious over the world
lifts me up today toward God?
Unhappy the man who relies
on men for his support!
Their glory flies, and disappears
in less time than the wake
of a vessel that plies the seas,
or than the quick arrow
that, far from the eye that guides it,
seeks the bird in the air.

The voice of immortal Wisdom
thunders, and instructs us.
"Children of man," it says,
"what is the fruit of your cares?
By what error, vain souls,
with the purest blood of your veins,
do you so often purchase
not the bread that restores you,
but a shadow that leaves you
more famished than before?

« Le pain que je vous propose Sert aux Anges d'aliment ; Dieu lui-même le compose De la fleur de son froment. C'est ce pain si délectable Que ne sert point à sa table Le monde que vous suivez. Je l'offre à qui me veut suivre. Approchez. Voulez-vous vivre ? Prenez, mangez, et vivez. »	"The bread that I offer you serves as food for the angels: God himself makes it from the flour of his wheat. This bread, so delectable, is not served at the table of the worldly ones you follow. I offer it to him who will follow me. Approach. Do you want to live? Take, eat, and live."
Ô Sagesse, ta parole Fit éclore l'univers, Posa sur un double pôle La terre au milieu des mers. Tu dis, et les cieux parurent, Et tous les astres coururent Dans leur ordre se placer. Avant les siècles tu règnes ; Et qui suis-je, que tu daignes Jusqu'à moi te rabaisser ?	O Wisdom, your word kindled the universe, placed on a double pole the earth in the midst of the seas. You spoke, and the heavens appeared, and all the stars raced to stand in their appointed order. Before the ages you reign, and who am I that you should deign to demean yourself before me?
Le Verbe, image du Père, Laissa son trône éternel, Et d'une mortelle mère Voulut naître homme et mortel. Comme l'orgueil fut le crime Dont il naissait la victime, Il dépouilla sa splendeur, Et vint, pauvre et misérable, Apprendre à l'homme coupable Sa véritable grandeur.	The Word, image of the Father, left his eternal throne, and of a mortal mother was born man and mortal. Since pride was the crime of which he was born the victim, he cast aside his splendor and came, poor and miserable, to teach guilty man his true grandeur.
L'âme heureusement captive Sous ton joug trouve la paix, Et s'abreuve d'une eau vive Qui ne s'épuise jamais. Chacun peut boire en cette onde ; Elle invite tout le monde ; Mais nous courons follement Chercher des sources bourbeuses Ou des citernes trompeuses D'où l'eau fuit à tout moment.	The soul who is happily captive beneath your yoke finds peace and drinks from living waters that never dry up. Each can drink from this flood; it invites everyone. But we run foolishly, to seek muddy springs or deceptive cisterns from which water flies every instant.

Notes

1. Collasse's setting has "tout vaincre et tout croire" instead of "tout vaincre, tout croire" (mm. 262–64, mm. 270–72).

2. Marchand's setting has "pourrons-nous" instead of "pourrai-je" at the repeat of this stanza (mm. 426–27).

3. Marchand's setting has "Les cantiques" instead of "Le cantique" and "nous" instead of "mes" at the repeat of this stanza (mm. 433–37).

Plate 1. Jean-Baptiste Moreau and Michel-Richard de Lalande, *Cantiques chantez devant le Roy* (Paris: Christophe Ballard, 1695), page 2. Paris, Bibliothèque nationale de France, Vm1 1168. Courtesy of the Bibliothèque nationale de France, Paris.

Plate 2. Pascal Collasse, *Cantiques spirituels, mis en musique* (Paris: Christophe Ballard, 1695), page 1. Paris, Bibliothèque nationale de France, Vm1 1624. Courtesy of the Bibliothèque nationale de France, Paris.

Plate 3. Duhalle, *Pseaumes et cantiques spirituels, mis en musique avec la basse-continue* (Paris: Christophe Ballard, 1695), page 38. Paris, Bibliothèque Sainte-Geneviève, Vm 22 RES. Courtesy of the Bibliothèque Sainte-Geneviève, Paris.

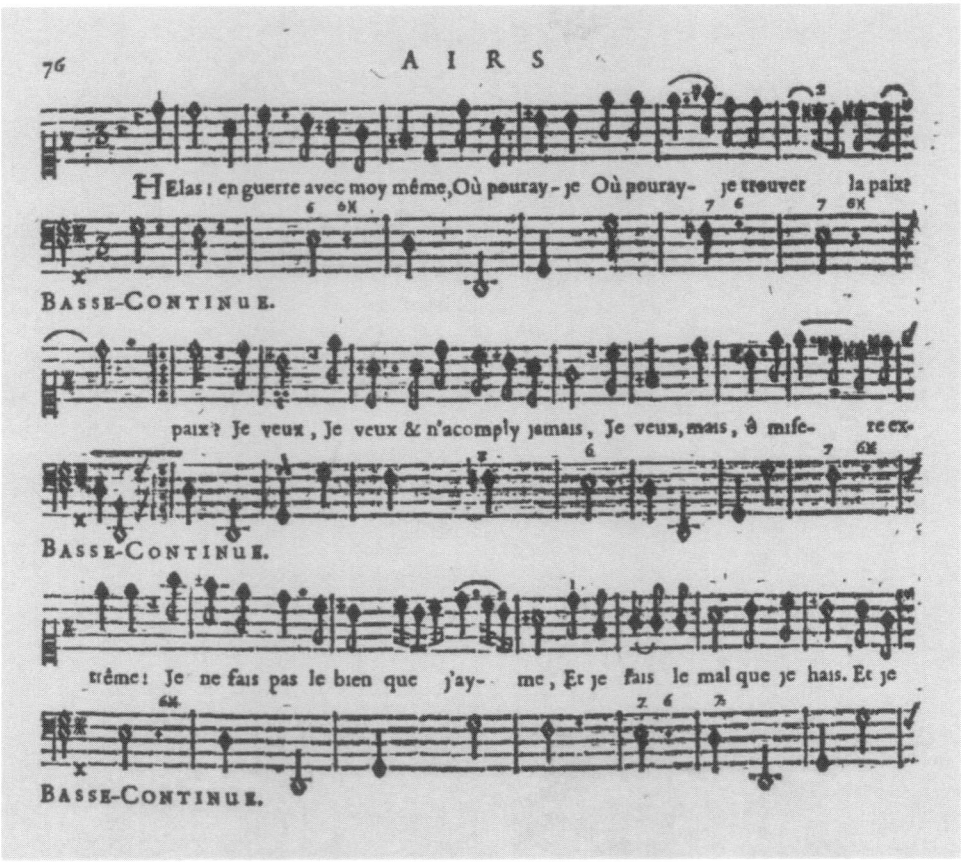

Plate 4. Jean-Baptiste du Bousset, "Hélas! en guerre avec moi-même," in *Airs spirituels des meilleurs autheurs, livre second* (Paris: Christophe Ballard, 1701), page 76. Paris, Bibliothèque nationale de France, Rés. 229 bis. Courtesy of the Bibliothèque nationale de France, Paris.

Plate 5. Jean-Noël Marchand, *Cantiques spirituels faits par M Racine pour estre mis en musique*, page 1. Paris, Bibliothèque nationale de France, Rés. 1262. Courtesy of the Bibliothèque nationale de France, Paris.

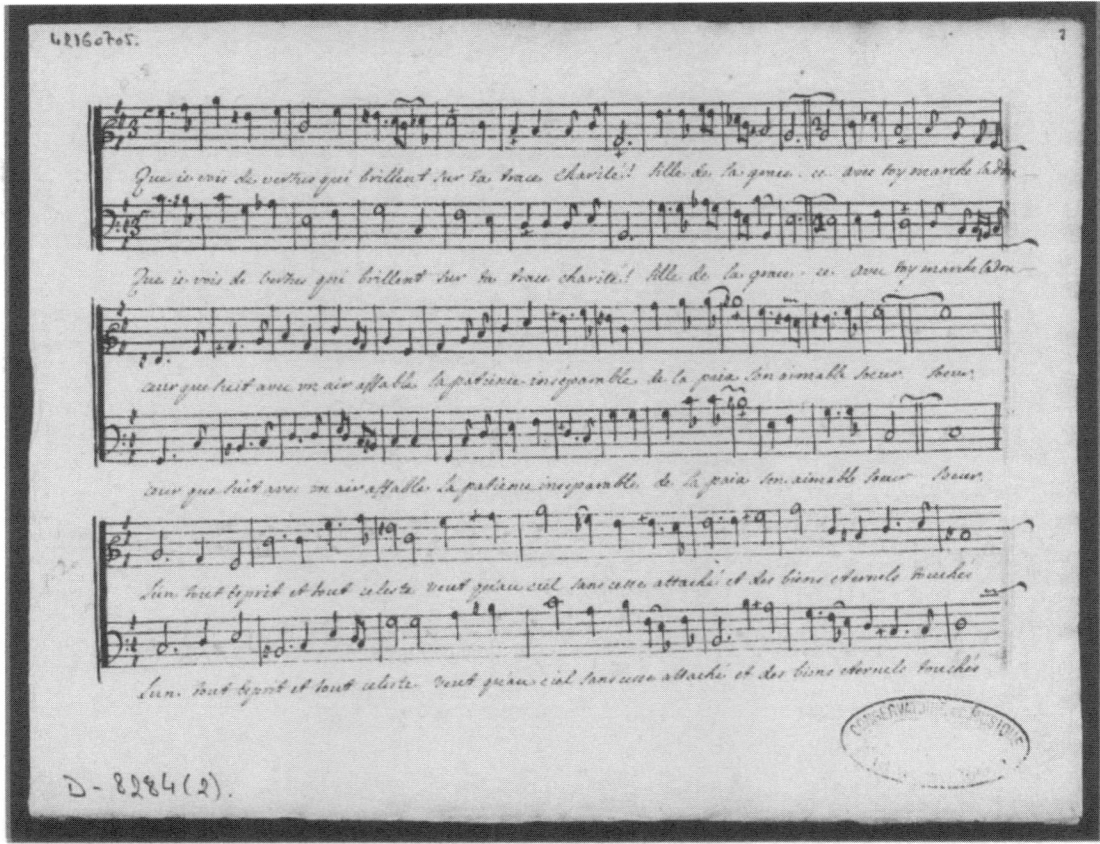

Plate 6. Jean-Baptiste Moreau, alternative setting of *Les méchants m'ont vanté*, stanza 6, included as a manuscript addition to end of Jean-Baptiste Moreau and Michel-Richard de Lalande, *Cantiques chantez devant le Roy* (Paris: Christophe Ballard, 1695). Paris, Bibliothèque nationale de France, D. 8284. Courtesy of the Bibliothèque nationale de France, Paris.

Jean-Baptiste Moreau
and Michel-Richard de Lalande

*Cantiques chantez
devant le Roy*

Les méchants m'ont vanté

Jean Racine, *Cantiques spirituels* I
Jean-Baptiste Moreau

For an alternative two-voice version of stanza 6 (mm. 69–89) and a three-voice version of stanza 12 (mm. 172–87), see the appendix.

96
-bres, Tel- le tu chas- ses d'un coup d'œil L'en- vie aux hu- mains si fa-
100
-ta- le, Et tou- te la trou- pe‿in- fer- na- le Des Vi- ces, en-
105
-fants de l'or- gueil, Des Vi- ces, en- fants de l'or- gueil.
Chœur
Li- bre d'am- bi- ti-
111
-on, sim- ple‿et sans ar- ti- fi- ce, Au- tant que tu hais l'in- jus- ti- ce, Au- tant la vé- ri- té te
114
plaît. Que peut la co- lè- re fa- rou- che Sur un cœur que ja- mais ne tou- che Le soin de
118
son pro- pre‿in- té- rêt?
[Seule]
Aux fai- bles- ses d'au- trui loin d'ê- tre‿in- ex- o- ra-

-ble, Tou- jours d'un voi- le fa- vo- ra- ble Tu t'ef- for- -ces de les cou-

-vrir. Quel tri- om- phe man- que à ta gloi- re? L'A- mour sait tout

vain- cre, tout croi- re, Tout es- pé- rer, et tout souf- frir.

Seule
Un jour Dieu ces- se- ra d'in- spi- rer des o- ra-

-cles; Le don des lan- gues, les mi- ra- cles, La sci- en- ce au-

-ra son dé- clin. -clin. L'A- mour, la Cha- ri- té di-

144
-vi- ne, É- ter- nel- - le en son o- ri- gi- ne, Ne con- naî-
148
-tra ja- mais de fin.
Chœur
Nos clar- tés i- ci- bas
153
ne sont qu'é- nig- mes som- - bres; Mais Dieu, sans voi- les et sans
158
om- bres, Nous é- clai- re- ra dans les cieux;
1.
2.
cieux; Et ce So-
162
-leil in- ac- ces- si- ble, Com- me à ses yeux je suis vi- si- ble, Se ren-
166
-dra vi- si- ble à mes yeux, Se ren- dra vi- si- ble à mes yeux.

Seule
L'A- mour sur tous les dons l'em- por- te a- vec jus- ti- -ce. De no- tre cé- les- te é- di- fi- ce La Foi vi- ve est le fon- de- -ment; La sain- te Es- pé- ran- ce l'é- lè- ve, L'ar- den- te Cha- ri- té l'a- -chè- ve Et l'as- su- re é- ter- nel- le- ment. Quand pour- rai- je t'of- -frir, ô Cha- ri- té su- prê- me, Au sein de la lu- miè- re mê- me, Le can- ti- que de mes sou- pirs; Et tou- jours brû-

Chœur

-lant pour ta gloi- re, Toujours puiser, et toujours boire Dans la sour--ce des vrais plaisirs, Et toujours brûlant pour ta gloi--re, Toujours puiser, toujours puiser, et toujours boire Dans la sour-ce des vrais plaisirs, des vrais plaisirs?

Mon Dieu, quelle guerre cruelle!

Jean Racine, *Cantiques spirituels* III

Jean-Baptiste Moreau

For alternative two-voice versions of stanzas 2 (mm. 19–40) and 4 (mm. 59–79), see the appendix.

Chœur

Ô grâce, ô rayon salutaire, Viens me mettre avec moi d'ac-cord; Et domptant par un doux effort Cet homme qui t'est si contraire, Fais ton esclave volontaire De cet esclave de la mort, Fais ton esclave volontaire De cet esclave de la mort.

Quel charme vainqueur du monde

Jean Racine, *Cantiques spirituels* IV

Jean-Baptiste Moreau

Quel char- me vain- queur du mon- de Vers Dieu m'é- lè- ve au- jour- d'hui? Mal- heu- reux l'hom- me qui fon- de Sur les hom- mes son ap- pui! Quel char- -pui! Leur gloi- re fuit, et s'ef- fa- ce En moins de temps que la tra- ce Du vais- seau qui fend les mers, Ou de la flè- che ra- pi- de Qui loin de l'œil qui la gui- de

laisse Plus af- fa- més que de- vant, Plus af- fa- més que de- vant?

7 6 — 6

Le pain que je vous pro- po- se Sert aux An- ges d'a- li-

[6] [—] [6]

-ment; Dieu lui- mê- me le com- po- se De la fleur de son fro- ment.

[—] [6] [6] [6] [#6] [6] [4 #] 1.

C'est ce pain si dé- lec- ta- ble Que ne sert point à sa ta- ble Le mon-

2. 6 ♮5 6 6 # 6

-de que vous sui- vez. Je l'of- fre à qui me veut sui- vre. Ap- pro-

#6 [4] [#] 6 7 6 — [—] 6

-chez. Vou- lez- vous vi- vre? Pre- nez, man- gez, et vi- vez, Pre-

7 6 6 6 [6] 6 6[—] [4 3] [—]
4 [3]

75
-nez, man- gez, et vi- vez.»
80
[Seule]
Ô Sa- ges- se, ta pa- ro- - le Fit é- clo- re l'u- ni-
84
-vers, Po- sa sur un dou- ble pô- le La ter- re au mi- lieu des mers. Tu
89
dis, et les cieux pa- ru- rent, Et tous les as- tres cou-
93
-ru- rent Dans leur or- dre se pla- cer.
1.
2.
-cer. A- vant les siè- cles tu
97
rè- gnes; Et qui suis- je, que tu dai- gnes Jus- qu'à moi te ra- bais- ser?

A- vant les siè- cles tu

Chœur
Le Verbe, i- ma- ge du Pè- re, Lais- sa son trô- ne é-ter- -nel, Et d'u- ne mor- tel- le mè- re Vou- lut naî- tre hom- me et mor- -tel. Com- me l'or- gueil fut le cri- me Dont il nais- sait la vic- -ti- me, Il dé- pouil- la sa splen- deur, Et vint, pau- vre et mi- sé- ra- ble, Ap- -pren- dre à l'hom- me cou- pa- ble Sa vé- ri- ta- ble gran- deur, Sa vé- ri-

-ta- ble gran- deur.

Seule, et Chœur en suite
L'â- me heu- reu- se- ment cap- ti- ve Sous ton joug trou- ve la paix, Et s'a-

-breu- ve d'u- ne eau vi- ve Qui ne s'é- pui- se ja- mais.

-mais. Cha- cun peut boi- re en cet- te on- de; El- le in- vi- te tout le

mon- de, Cha- cun peut boi- re en cet- te on- de; Mais nous cou- rons, nous cou- rons fol- le-

-ment Cher- cher des sour- ces bour- beu- ses Ou des ci- ter- nes trom-

Heureux qui, de la sagesse

Jean Racine, *Cantiques spirituels* II
Michel-Richard de Lalande

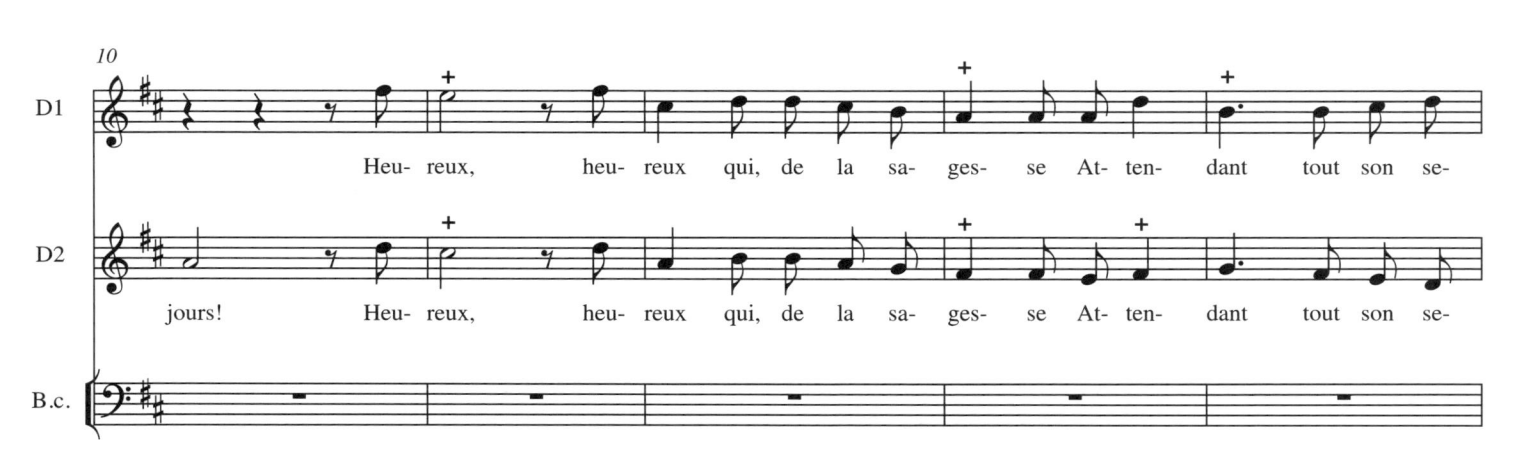

-peu- ses D'où l'eau fuit à tout mo- ment, D'où l'eau fuit à tout mo- ment.

[Dessus 1]
[Dessus 2] Heu- reux, heu- reux qui, de la sa- ges- se At- ten- dant tout son se-
Basse continue

-cours, N'a point mis en la ri- ches- se L'es- poir de ses der- niers

jours! Heu- reux, heu- reux qui, de la sa- ges- se At- ten- dant tout son se-

Heu- reux, heu- reux qui, de la sa- ges- se At- ten- dant tout son se-

For alternative versions of stanzas 3 (mm. 79–106), 4 (mm. 107–32), and 5 (mm. 133–57), see the appendix.

22

-cours, N'a point mis en la ri- ches- se L'es- poir de ses der- niers jours!

-cours, N'a point mis en la ri- ches- se L'es- poir de ses der- niers jours! La mort n'a rien qui l'é- ton- ne; Et dès que son Dieu l'or-

-don- ne, Son â- me pre- nant l'es- sor S'é- lè- ve d'un vol ra-

-pi- de Vers la de- meu- re où ré- si- de Son vé- ri- ta- ble tré-

La mort n'a rien qui l'étonne; Et dès que son Dieu l'ordonne, Son âme prenant l'essor S'élève d'un vol rapide Vers la demeure où réside Son véritable trésor.

De quelle douleur profonde Seront un jour péné-

-trés Ces in- sen- sés qui du mon- de, Sei- gneur, vi- vent en i-
-vrés, -vrés, Quand, par u- ne fin sou- dai- ne Dé- trom-
-pés d'u- ne om- bre vai- ne, Qui pas- se et ne re- vient plus, Leurs yeux du
fond de l'a- bî- me Près de ton trô- ne su- bli- me Ver- ront bril-
-ler tes é- lus! Quand, par u- ne fin sou-
-lus! «In- for- tu- nés que nous som- mes, Où s'é- ga- raient nos es-

-prits? Voi- là, di- ront- ils, ces hom- mes, Vils ob- jets de nos mé- pris.

-pris. Leur sain- te et pé- ni- ble vi- e Nous pa- rut u- ne fo-

-li- e; Mais au- jour- d'hui tri- om- phants, Le

Gravement

ciel chan- te leur lou- an- ge Et Dieu lui- mê- me les

ran- ge Au nom- bre de ses en- fants. Leur -fants.

Pour trou- ver un bien fra- gi- le Qui nous vient d'ê- tre ar- ra-

D2
B.c.
111
-ché, Par quel che- min dif- fi- ci- le Hé- las! nous a- vons mar- ché!
115
Pour trou- -ché! Dans u- ne rou- te͜ in- sen- sé- e No- tre͜ â- me͜ en vain s'est las-
120
Gravement
-sé- e, Sans se re- po- ser ja- mais, Fer- mant
124
l'œil à la lu- miè- re Qui nous mon- trait la car- riè- re De
129
la bien- heu- reu- se paix. Dans u- ne paix. De
134
nos at- ten- tats in- jus- tes Quel fruit nous est- il re- sté? Où sont les ti- tres au-

-gus- tes Dont no- tre or- gueil s'est flat- té? De- -té? Sans a-

-mis et sans dé- fen- se, Au trô- ne de la ven- gean- ce Ap- pe-

-lés en ju- ge- ment, **Gravement** Fai- bles et tris- tes vic- ti-

-mes, Nous y ve- nons de nos cri- mes Ac- com- pa- gnés seu- le-

-ment. Sans a- -ment.» Ain- si, d'u- ne voix plain- ti-

-ve, Ex- pri- me- ra ses re- mords La pé- ni- ten- ce tar-

28

-di- ve Des in- con- so- la- bles morts. Ain-
morts. Ce qui fai- sait leurs dé- li- ces, Sei- gneur, fe- ra leurs sup-
-pli- ces; Et par u- ne_é- ga- le loi Tes saints trou- ve- ront des
char- mes Dans le sou- ve- nir des lar- mes Qu'ils
ver- - sent i- ci pour toi. Ce qui fai- toi.

Gravement

Pascal Collasse

*Cantiques spirituels
mis en musique*

Les méchants m'ont vanté

Jean Racine, *Cantiques spirituels* I

Pascal Collasse

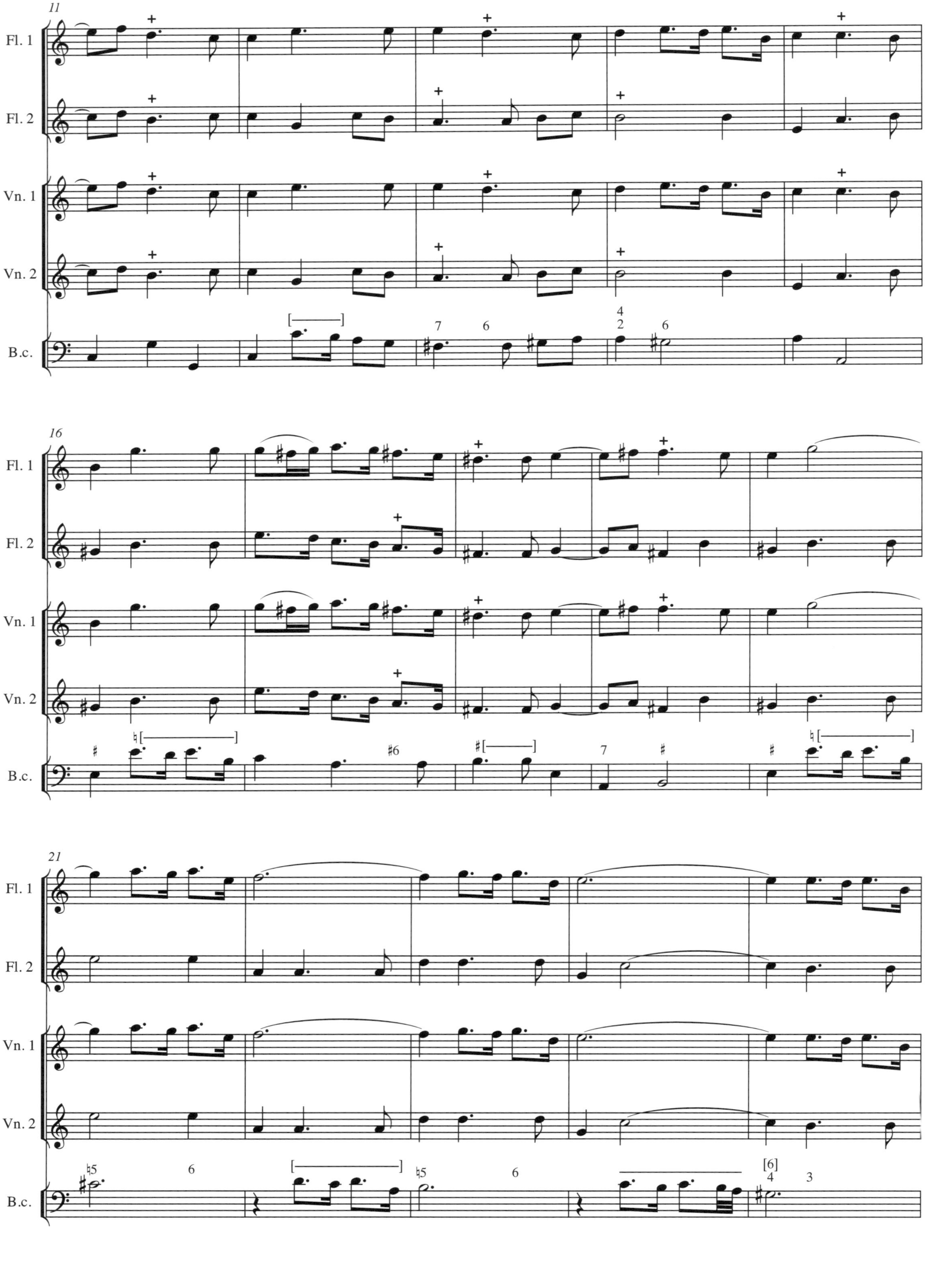
11
Fl. 1
Fl. 2
Vn. 1
Vn. 2
B.c.
16
Fl. 1
Fl. 2
Vn. 1
Vn. 2
B.c.
21
Fl. 1
Fl. 2
Vn. 1
Vn. 2
B.c.

-chants m'ont van- té leurs men- son- ges fri- vo- les; Mais je n'ai- me que les pa-

[Seule] Les mé-

-ro- les De l'é- ter- nel- le Vé- ri- té. Les mé- -té.

Plein du feu di- vin qui m'in- spi- re, Je con- sa- cre au- jour- d'hui ma

ly- re À la cé- les- te Cha- ri- té. -té. En vain je par- le-

-rais le lan- ga- ge des an- ges; En vain, mon Dieu, de tes lou-

-an- ges Je rem- pli- rais tout l'u- ni- vers: En

-vers: Sans a- mour, ma gloi- re n'é- ga- le Que la gloi- re de la cym-

35

36

D1: -mes Des mys- tè- res les plus su- bli- mes, Et de li- re dans l'a ve- nir? Sans amour, ma sci- en- ce est vai- ne Com- me le son- ge dont à pei- ne Il res- te un lé- ger sou- ve- nir. Sans amour, ma sci- en- ce est vai- ne Com- me le son- ge dont à pei- ne Il res- te un lé- ger sou- ve-

D2: -mes Des mys- tè- res les plus su- bli- mes, Et de li- re dans l'a ve- nir? Sans amour, ma sci- en- ce est vai- ne Com- me le son- ge dont à pei- ne Il res- te un lé- ger sou- ve-

37

Symphonie
Très lentement

Que me sert que ma foi trans-por- -te les mon- ta- gnes,

Que me sert que ma foi trans-por- -te les mon- ta- gnes,

Que me sert que ma foi trans-por- -te les mon- ta- gnes,

39

Que dans les a- ri- des cam- pa- gnes Les tor- rents nais- sent sous mes pas, Ou que ra- ni- mant la pous- siè- re, El- le rende aux morts la lumière Si l'amour ne l'anime pas?

Symphonie
Très lentement

42

le nom chrétien, Bravant les croix les plus infâmes, Je livrerais mon corps aux flammes, Si je n'aime, je ne suis rien, Si je n'aime, si je n'aime, je ne suis rien.

Que je vois de Vertus qui brillent sur ta trace, Charité, fille de la Grâce! Avec toi marche la Douceur, Que suit, avec un air affable, La Patience inséparable De la Paix, son aimable

soeur. Tel que l'as- tre du jour é- car- te les Té- nè- bres, De la Nuit com-
-pa- gnes fu- nè- bres, Tel- le tu chas- ses d'un coup d'œil L'en-
-vie aux hu- mains si fa- ta- le, Et tou- te la trou- pe in- fer- na- le Des
Vi- ces, en- fants de l'or- gueil. Li- bre d'am- bi- tion,

46

D1: simple, et sans artifice, Autant que tu hais l'injustice, Autant la vérité te plaît. Que peut la colère farouche Sur un cœur que jamais ne touche Le soin de son propre intérêt?

D1, D2, D3 (Récit): Aux faiblesses d'autrui loin d'être inexorable, Toujours d'un voile favorable Tu t'efforces de les couvrir.

Lyrics:

D1, D2, D3: Tous Aux fai- bles- ses d'au- trui loin d'ê- tre in- ex- o- ra- ble, Tou- jours d'un voi- le fa- vo- ra- ble Tu t'ef- for- ces de les cou- vrir.

D1: Récit — Quel tri-

48

267

-frir. Quel tri- om- phe, quel tri- om- phe, quel tri- om- phe man- que à ta gloi-

Tous -frir. Quel tri- om- phe, quel tri- om- phe man- que à ta gloi-

Tous -frir. Quel tri- om- phe, quel tri- om- phe man- que à ta gloi-

270

-re? L'A- mour sait tout vain- cre et tout croi- re, Tout es- pé-

-re? L'A- mour sait tout vain- cre et tout croi- re,

-re? L'A- mour sait tout vain- cre et tout croi- re,

Symphonie
Très lentement

D1: -rer, tout es- pé- rer, et tout souf- frir.

D2: Tout es- pé- rer, et tout souf- frir.

D3: Tout es- pé- rer, et tout souf- frir.

282
Fl. 1
Fl. 2
Vn. 1
Vn. 2
B.c.
288
Fl. 1
Fl. 2
Vn. 1
Vn. 2
B.c.
294
Fl. 1
Fl. 2
Vn. 1
Vn. 2
B.c.

52

jour Dieu ces- se- ra d'in- spi- rer des o- ra- cles;

Le don des lan- gues, les mi- ra- cles, La sci- en- ce au- ra son dé- clin. L'A- mour,

la Cha- ri- té di- vi- ne, É- ter- nel- le en son o- ri- gi- ne, Ne con- naî-

-tra ja- mais de fin, L'A- mour, la Cha- ri- té di- vi- ne, É- ter-

-nel- le en son o- ri- gi- ne, Ne con- naî- tra ja- mais de fin. Nos clar- tés i- ci-

-bas ne sont qu'é- nig- mes som- bres; Mais Dieu, sans voi- les et sans

54

om- bres, Nous é- clai- re- ra dans les cieux; cieux;

Et ce So- leil in- ac- ces- si- ble, Com- me à ses yeux je suis vi-

-si- ble, Se ren- dra vi- si- ble à mes yeux, Et ce So- leil in- ac- ces-

-si- ble, Com- me à ses yeux je suis vi- si- ble, Se ren- dra vi-

Gai

-si- ble à mes yeux. L'A- mour sur tous les dons l'em- por- te a- vec jus-

L'A- mour sur tous les dons l'em- por- te a- vec jus-

-ti- ce. De no- tre cé- les- te é- di- fi- ce La Foi

-ti- ce. De no- tre cé- les- te é- di- fi- ce La Foi

vi- ve est le fon- de- ment; La sain- te Es- pé- ran- ce l'é-
lè- ve, L'ar- den- te Cha- ri- té l'a- chè- ve Et l'as- su- re é-
-ter- nel- le- ment, Et l'as- su- re é- ter- nel- le- ment.

Symphonie
Très lentement

396
Fl. 1
Fl. 2
Vn. 1
Vn. 2
B.c.
401
Fl. 1
Fl. 2
Vn. 1
Vn. 2
B.c.
406
Fl. 1
Fl. 2
Vn. 1
Vn. 2
B.c.

57

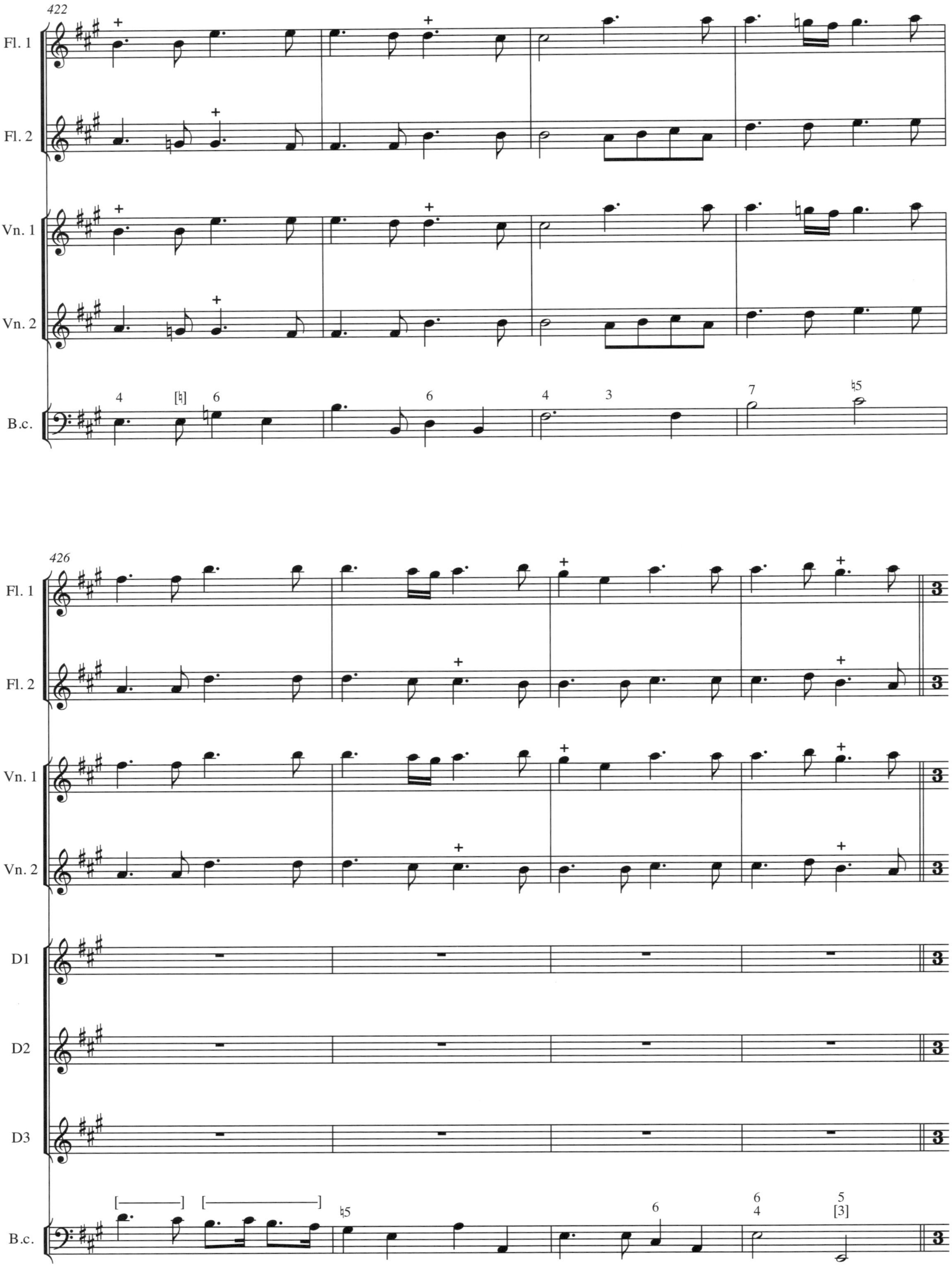
422
Fl. 1
Fl. 2
Vn. 1
Vn. 2
B.c.
426
Fl. 1
Fl. 2
Vn. 1
Vn. 2
D1
D2
D3
B.c.

Quand pourrai-je t'offrir, ô Charité suprême, Au sein de la lumière même, Le cantique de mes sou-

Chœur
Doux

-pirs; Tous Quand pour- rai- je t'of- frir, ô Cha- ri- té su-

-rê- me, Au sein de la lu- miè- re mê- me, Le can- ti- que

61

Fl. 1
Fl. 2
Vn. 1
Vn. 2
D1
D2
D3
B.c.
Chœur
Tous
-sirs? Et tou- jours brû- lant pour ta gloi- re Tou- jours pui-
-ser, et tou- jours boi- re Dans la sour- ce des vrais plai- sirs?

Heureux qui, de la sagesse

Jean Racine, *Cantiques spirituels* II

Pascal Collasse

Symphonie
Très lentement

Heu- reux, heu- reux qui, de la sa- ges- se At- ten-

-dant tout son se- cours, N'a point mis en la ri- ches- se L'es- poir de ses der- niers jours! La mort n'a rien qui l'é- ton- ne; Et dès que son Dieu l'or- -don- ne, Son â- me pre- nant l'es- sor S'é- lè- ve d'un vol ra- -pi- de Vers la de- meu- re où ré- si- de Son vé- ri- ta- ble tré- sor.

Lentement

De quel- le dou- leur pro- fon- de Se- ront un

De quel- le dou- leur pro- fon- de Se- ront un

83
D1
yeux du fond de l'a- bî- me Près de ton trô- ne su- bli- me Ver-
D2
yeux du fond de l'a- bî- me Près de ton trô- ne su- bli- me Ver-
B.c.
86
Récit
D1
-ront bril- ler tes é- lus! «In- for- tu- nés que nous som- mes,
Récit
D2
-ront bril- ler tes é- lus! «In- for- tu- nés que nous som- mes,
Récit
D3
«In- for- tu- nés que nous som- mes,
B.c.
91
Fl. 1
Vn. 1
Fl. 2
Vn. 2
Tous
D1
Où s'é- ga- raient nos es- prits? In- for- tu- nés que nous som- mes,
Tous
D2
Où s'é- ga- raient nos es- prits? In- for- tu- nés que nous som- mes,
Tous
D3
Où s'é- ga- raient nos es- prits? In- for- tu- nés que nous som- mes,
B.c.

96
Fl. 1
Vn. 1
Fl. 2
Vn. 2
D1
D2
D3
B.c.
Récit
Où s'é- ga- raient nos es- prits? Voi- là, di- ront- ils, ces hom- mes, Vils ob-
Où s'é- ga- raient nos es- prits?
Où s'é- ga- raient nos es- prits?
100
-jets de nos mé- pris. Leur sain- te et pé- ni- ble vi- e Nous pa- rut u- ne fo-
Récit
Leur sain- te et pé- ni- ble vi- e Nous pa- rut u- ne fo-
Récit
Leur sain- te et pé- ni- ble vi- e Nous pa- rut u- ne fo-

-lie; Mais aujourd'hui triomphants, Le ciel chante leur lou-

-ange Et Dieu lui-même les range Au nombre de ses en-

-fants, Mais aujourd'hui triomphants, Le ciel chante leur louange Et Dieu lui-même les range Au nombre de ses enfants.

Symphonie
Très lentement

Pour trou- ver un bien fra- gi- le Qui nous vient d'ê- tre ar- ra- -ché, Par quel che- min dif- fi- ci- le Hé- las! nous a- vons mar- -ché! Pour trou- -ché! Dans u- ne rou- te in- sen- sé- e No- -tre âme en vain s'est las- sé- e, Sans se re- po- ser ja- mais, Fer- mant l'œil à la lu- -miè- re Qui nous mon- trait la car- riè- re De la bien- heu- reu- se paix.

73

De nos attentats injustes Quel fruit nous est-il resté? Où sont les titres augustes Dont notre orgueil s'est flatté? De-té? Sans amis et sans défense, Au trône de la vengeance Appelés en jugement, Faibles et tristes victimes, Nous y venons de nos crimes Accompa-

194
D1
-gnés seu- le- ment. Fai- bles et tris- tes vic- ti- mes,
D2
Fai- bles et tris- tes vic- ti- mes,
B.c.
199
D1
Nous y ve- nons de nos cri- mes Ac- com- pa- gnés seu- le-
D2
Nous y ve- nons de nos cri- mes Ac- com- pa- gnés seu- le-
B.c.
Lentement
203
Récit
D1
-ment.» Ain- si, d'u- ne voix plain- ti- - ve, Ex- pri- me- ra ses re-
Récit
D2
-ment.» Ain- si, d'u- ne voix plain- ti- - ve, Ex- pri- me- ra ses re-
Récit
D3
Ain- si, d'u- ne voix plain- ti- - ve, Ex- pri- me- ra ses re-
B.c.
208
D1
-mords La pé- ni- ten- ce tar- di- ve Des in- con- so- la- bles
D2
-mords La pé- ni- ten- ce tar- di- ve Des in- con- so- la- bles
D3
-mords La pé- ni- ten- ce tar- di- - ve Des in- con- so- la- bles
B.c.

morts. Ain- si, d'u- ne voix plain- ti- ve, Ex- pri- me- ra ses re-
-mords La pé- ni- ten- ce tar- di- ve Des in- con- so- la- bles morts.

Récit
Ce qui fai- sait leurs dé- li- ces, Sei- gneur, fe- ra leurs sup-

76

226

D1: -pli- ces; Et par u- ne é- ga- le loi Tes saints trou- ve- ront des char- mes

D2: *Récit* Et par u- ne é- ga- le loi Tes saints trou- ve- ront des char- mes

D3: *Récit* Et par u- ne é- ga- le loi Tes saints trou- ve- ront des char- mes

B.c.

232

D1: Dans le sou- ve- nir des lar- mes Qu'ils ver-

D2: Dans le sou- ve- nir des lar- mes Qu'ils ver-

D3: Dans le sou- ve- nir, Dans le sou- ve- nir des

B.c.

236

D1: -sent i- ci pour toi, Et par u- ne é- ga- le loi Tes

D2: -sent i- ci pour toi,

D3: lar- mes Qu'ils ver- -sent, qu'ils ver-

B.c.

240
Fl. 1
Vn. 1
Fl. 2
Vn. 2
D1
Tous
saints trou- ve- ront des char- mes, Et par u- ne é- ga- le
D2
Tous
Et par u- ne é- ga- le
D3
Tous
- sent i- ci pour toi, Et par u- ne é- ga- le
B.c.
244
loi Tes saints trou- ve- ront des char- mes Dans le sou- ve-
loi Tes saints trou- ve- ront des char- mes Dans le sou- ve-
loi Tes saints trou- ve- ront des char- mes Dans le sou- ve-

249
Fl. 1
Vn. 1
Fl. 2
Vn. 2
D1
-nir des lar- mes Qu'ils ver- - - sent i- ci pour
D2
-nir des lar- mes Qu'ils ver- - - sent i- ci pour
D3
-nir des lar- mes Qu'ils ver- - sent i- ci pour
B.c.

254
Fl. 1
Vn. 1
Fl. 2
Vn. 2
D1
toi, Et par u- ne é- ga- le loi Tes saints trou- ve- ront des char- mes Dans le sou- ve-
D2
toi, Et par u- ne é- ga- le loi Tes saints trou- ve- ront des char- mes Dans le sou- ve-
D3
toi, Tes saints trou- ve- ront des char- mes Dans le sou- ve- nir des lar- mes Qu'ils
B.c.

-nir des lar- mes Qu'ils ver- - sent i- ci pour toi.

Mon Dieu, quelle guerre cruelle!

Jean Racine, *Cantiques spirituels* III

Pascal Collasse

81

Mon Dieu, quelle guerre cruelle! Je trouve deux hommes en moi; L'un veut que plein d'amour pour toi Mon cœur te soit toujours fidèle. L'autre à tes volontés rebelle Me ré-

-volte contre ta loi. L'un tout esprit, et tout céleste, Veut qu'au ciel sans cesse attaché, Et des biens éternels touché, Je compte pour rien tout le reste; Et l'autre par son poids funeste Me tient vers la terre penché. Hélas! en guerre avec moi-même, Où pourrai-je trouver la paix? Hé- paix? Je veux, et n'ac-com-plis ja- mais. Je veux, mais, ô mi-sè-re ex-trê- me!

Je ne fais pas le bien que j'ai- me, Et je fais le mal que je hais,

Je ne fais pas le bien que j'ai- me, Et je fais le mal que je

Très lentement

hais. Ô grâ- ce, ô ray- on sa- lu- tai- re, Viens me

Ô grâ- ce, ô ray- on sa- lu- tai- re, Viens me

Ô grâ- ce, ô ray- on sa- lu- tai- re, Viens me

met- tre a- vec moi d'ac- cord, Viens me met- tre a- vec moi d'ac-

met- tre a- vec moi d'ac- cord, Viens me met- tre a- vec moi d'ac-

met- tre a- vec moi d'ac- cord, Viens me met- tre a- vec moi d'ac-

85

-ptant par un doux effort Cet homme qui t'est si contraire,

Fais ton esclave volontaire De cet esclave de la

D1, D2, D3: mort. Et domptant par un doux effort Cet homme qui t'est si contraire,

D1, D2, D3: Fais ton esclave volontaire De cet esclave de la

131
[Tous]
Fl. 1
[Tous]
Fl. 2
Vn. 1
Vn. 2
D1
mort, Fais ton es- cla- ve vo- lon- tai- re De cet es-
D2
mort, Fais ton es- cla- ve vo- lon- tai- re De cet es-
D3
mort, Fais ton es- cla- ve vo- lon- tai- re De cet es-
B.c.
♯ ♯[——] 7 6 ♯6[——] 6[——]
136
Fl. 1
Fl. 2
Vn. 1
Vn. 2
D1
-cla- ve, de cet es- cla- ve de la mort.
D2
-cla- ve, de cet es- cla- ve de la mort.
D3
-cla- ve, de cet es- cla- ve de la mort.
B.c.
5 6 7 6 6 4 5 ♯ ♮

Quel charme vainqueur du monde

Jean Racine, *Cantiques spirituels* IV

Pascal Collasse

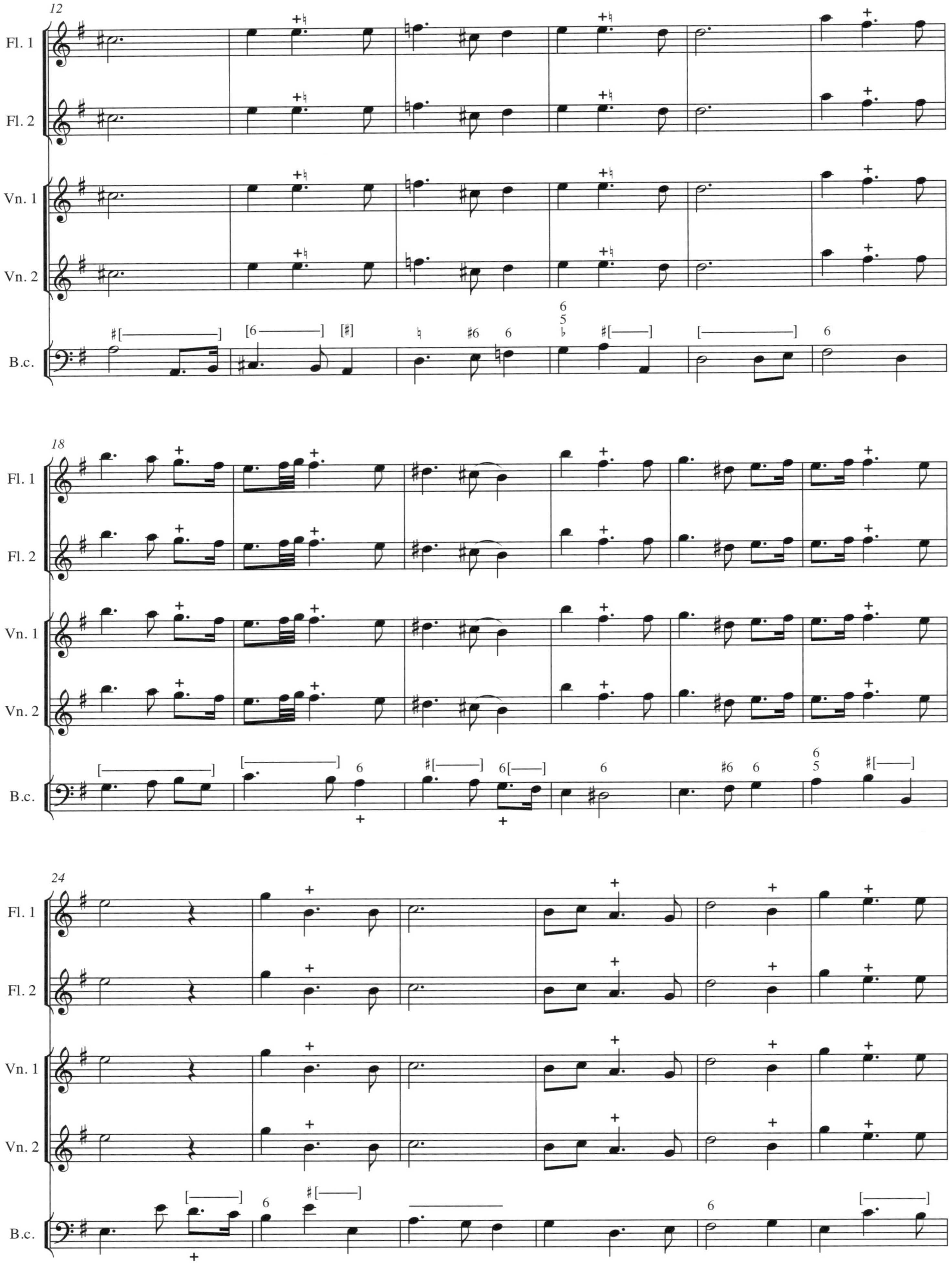
12
Fl. 1
Fl. 2
Vn. 1
Vn. 2
B.c.
18
Fl. 1
Fl. 2
Vn. 1
Vn. 2
B.c.
24
Fl. 1
Fl. 2
Vn. 1
Vn. 2
B.c.

30
Fl. 1
Fl. 2
Vn. 1
Vn. 2
D1
B.c.
Seul
Seul
Quel char- me vain- queur du mon- de
36
Vers Dieu m'é- lè- ve au- jour- d'hui? Mal- heu- reux l'hom- me qui
42
fon- de Sur les hom- - mes son ap- pui! Leur gloi- re fuit, et s'ef-

48
Vn. 1
Vn. 2
D1
-fa- ce En moins de temps que la tra- ce Du vais- seau qui fend les
B.c.
53
Vn. 1
Vn. 2
D1
mers, Ou de la flè- che ra- pi- de Qui loin de l'œil qui la
B.c.
57
Vn. 1
Vn. 2
D1
gui- de Cher- che l'oi- seau dans les airs. De la Sa- ges- se im- mor-
D2
De la Sa- ges- se im- mor-
B.c.
6

-tel- le La voix ton- ne, et nous in- struit. «En- fants des hom- mes, dit- el- le, De vos soins quel est le fruit? Par quel- le er- reur, â- mes vai- nes, Du plus pur sang de vos vei- nes A- che- tez- vous si sou- vent, Non un pain qui vous re- pais- se, Mais u-

*From this point through m. 113, the source does not specify whether this part is assigned to Vn. 1 or Vn. 2. See "Notes on Performance" in the introduction.

ne sert point à sa table Le monde que vous suivez. Je l'offre à qui me veut suivre. Approchez. Voulez-vous vivre? Prenez, mangez, et vivez, Voulez-vous vivre? Prenez, man-

-gez, et vi- vez.»

Fl. 1
Fl. 2
Vn. 1
Vn. 2
D1
B.c.
Doux
Seul
Seul
Ô Sa- ges- se, ô Sa- -ges- se, ta pa- ro- le Fit é- clo- re l'u- ni- vers, ta pa- ro- le Fit é-

-clore l'univers, Posa sur un double pôle La terre au milieu des mers. Tu dis, et les cieux parurent, Et tous les astres coururent Dans leur ordre se placer. Avant les siècles tu rè- gnes; Et qui suis- je, que tu dai- gnes Jus- qu'à moi te ra- bais- ser, Et qui

suis- je, et qui suis- je, que tu dai- gnes Jus- qu'à moi te ra- bais- ser?

Seule
Ô___ Sa- ges- se, ô Sa- ges- se, ta pa- ro- le Fit é- clo- re l'u- ni- vers,___

Seule
Ô___ Sa- ges- se, ô Sa- ges- se, ta pa- ro- le Fit é- clo- re, fit é-

Seule
Ô___ Sa- ges- se, ô Sa- ges- se, ta pa- ro- le Fit é- clo- re l'u- ni- vers,

176
Fl. 1
Fl. 2
Vn. 1
Vn. 2
D1
D2
D3
B.c.
Tous
[Tous]
Tous
[Tous]
Tous
— ta pa- ro- le Fit é- clo- re l'u- ni- vers, Ô Sa- ges- se, ô Sa-
Tous
-clo- re l'u- ni- vers, ta pa- ro- le Fit é- clo- re l'u- ni- vers, Ô Sa-
Tous
— ta pa- ro- le Fit é- clo- re l'u- ni- vers, Ô Sa- ges- se, ô Sa-
181
Fl. 1
Fl. 2
Vn. 1
Vn. 2
D1
D2
D3
B.c.
Récit
-ges- se, ta pa- ro- le Fit é- clo- re l'u- ni- vers, Po-
Récit
-ges- se, ta pa- ro- le Fit é- clo- re l'u- ni- vers, Po-
Récit
-ges- se, ta pa- ro- le Fit é- clo- re l'u- ni- vers, Po- sa sur un dou- ble

-sa sur un dou- ble pô- le La ter- re au mi- lieu des mers. Tu

-sa sur un dou- ble pô- le La ter- re au mi- lieu des mers. Tu

pô- le La ter- re au mi- lieu des mers. Tu dis, et les cieux pa-

dis, et les cieux pa- ru- rent, Et tous les as- tres cou- ru- rent Dans leur or- dre se pla-

dis, et les cieux pa- ru- rent, Et tous les as- tres cou- ru- rent Dans leur or- dre se pla-

-ru- rent, Et tous les as- tres cou- ru- rent Dans leur or- dre se pla- cer.

196
Fl. 1
Fl. 2
Vn. 1
Vn. 2
D1
D2
D3
B.c.
Tous
-cer. A- vant les
Tous
-cer. A- vant les siè- cles tu rè- gnes, A- vant les
Tous
A-vant les siè- cles tu rè- gnes, A- vant les siè- cles tu
201
siè- cles tu rè- gnes, tu rè- gnes, A- vant les siè- cles tu rè- gnes;
siè- cles tu rè- gnes, tu rè- gnes, A- vant les siè- cles tu rè- gnes;
rè- - gnes, tu rè- - gnes, tu rè- gnes;

206
Fl. 1
Fl. 2
Vn. 1
Vn. 2
D1
D2
D3
B.c.
Récit
Et qui suis- je, que tu dai- gnes Jus- qu'à moi te ra- bais- ser,
Récit
Et qui
212
Tous
Et qui
Tous
suis- je, et qui suis- je, que tu dai- gnes Jus- qu'à moi te ra- bais- ser, Et qui
Tous
Et qui

suis- je, et qui suis- je, que tu dai- gnes Jus- qu'à moi te ra- bais- ser? Le Ver- be, i- ma- ge du Père, Lais- sa son trô- ne é- ter- nel, Et d'u- ne mor- tel- le mè- re Vou- lut naî- tre homme et mor- tel. Comme l'or- gueil fut le cri- me Dont il nais- sait la vic- ti- me, Il dé- pouil- la sa splen- deur, Et

Très lentement
Doux

vint, pau- vre et mi- sé- ra- ble, Ap- pren- dre à l'hom- me cou- pa- ble Sa vé- ri- ta- ble gran- deur, Et vint, pau- vre et mi- sé- ra- ble, Ap- pren- dre à l'hom- me cou- pa- ble Sa vé- ri- ta- ble gran- deur. L'â- me heu- reu- se- ment cap- ti- ve Sous ton joug trou- ve la paix, Et s'a- breu- ve d'u- ne eau vi- ve Qui ne s'é-

-puise jamais. Chacun peut boire en cette onde;

Elle invite tout le monde; Mais nous courons follement

Chercher des sources bourbeuses Ou des ci-

107

-ter- nes trom- peu- ses D'où l'eau fuit à tout mo- ment.

Chœur
Très lentement

Tous
L'â- me heu- reu- se- ment cap- ti- ve Sous ton joug

Tous
L'â- me heu- reu- se- ment cap- ti- ve Sous ton joug

Tous
L'â- me heu- reu- se- ment cap- ti- ve Sous ton joug

108

D1: trou- ve la paix, Et s'a- breu- ve d'u- ne eau vi- ve Qui ne s'é-
D2: trou- ve la paix, Et s'a- breu- ve d'u- ne eau vi- ve Qui ne s'é-
D3: trou- ve la paix, Et s'a- breu- ve d'u- ne eau vi- ve Qui ne s'é-

B.c. figures: 6[——] 7 ♭6 [♭]7

D1: -pui- se ja- mais. *Récit* Cha- cun peut boi- re en cet- te on- de;
D2: -pui- se ja- mais. *Récit* Cha- cun peut boi- re en cet- te on- de; El- le in-
D3: -pui- se ja- mais.

B.c. figures: 7 7 6 ♯[——] 7 ♯5 ♮ [♮5] [♮6] [——]

109

-de; El- le in- vi- te, el- le in- vi- te tout le mon- de; Mais nous cou-rons ___ fol- le- ment Cher- cher des sour- ces bour- beu- ses Ou des ci- ter- nes trom-

111

-peu- ses D'où l'eau fuit à tout mo- ment, D'où l'eau fuit à tout mo- ment, D'où

-beu- ses Ou des ci- ter- nes trom- peu- ses D'où l'eau fuit, d'où l'eau fuit à tout mo-

-beu- ses Ou des ci- ter- nes trom- peu- ses D'où l'eau fuit à tout mo- ment, D'où

l'eau fuit à tout mo- ment, D'où l'eau fuit à tout mo- ment.

-ment, D'où l'eau fuit à tout mo- ment, à tout mo- ment, à tout mo- ment.

l'eau fuit à tout mo- ment, D'où l'eau fuit à tout mo- ment, à tout mo- ment.

Jean-Noël Marchand

*Cantiques spirituels
faits par M Racine*

Les méchants m'ont vanté

Jean Racine, *Cantiques spirituels* I

Jean-Noël Marchand

*All basse continue figures in this piece are editorial.

Les mé- chants m'ont van- té leurs men- son- ges fri- vo- les; Mais je n'ai- me que les pa- ro- les De l'é- ter- nel- le Vé- ri- té.

-té. Plein du feu divin qui m'inspire, Je consacre au jour d'hui ma lyre À la céleste Charité, Plein du feu divin qui m'inspire, Je consacre au jour d'hui ma lyre À la céleste Charité.

Ritournelle

En vain je parlerais le lan-

-ga- ge des an- ges; En vain, mon Dieu, de tes lou- an- ges Je rem- pli- rais tout l'u- ni- vers: En -vers: Sans a- mour, ma gloi- re n'é- ga- le Que la gloi- re de la cym- ba- le Qui d'un vain bruit frap- pe les airs, Sans a- mour, ma gloi- re n'é- ga- le Que la gloi- re de la cym- ba- le Qui d'un vain bruit frap- pe les airs. Sans a- airs.

Prélude

Que sert à mon es- prit de per- cer les a- bî- mes Des mys-

119

songe dont à peine Il reste un léger souvenir. Que me sert que ma foi transporte les montagnes, Que dans les arides campagnes Les torrents naissent sous mes pas, Ou que ranimant la poussière, Elle rende aux morts la lumière Si l'amour ne l'anime pas? Que me sert que ma foi transporte les mon-

-ta- gnes, Que dans les a- ri- des cam- pa- gnes Les tor- rents nais- sent sous mes pas, Ou que ra- ni- mant la pous- siè- re, El- le rend aux morts la lu- miè- re Si l'a- mour, si l'a- mour ne l'a- ni- me pas, Si l'a- mour, si l'a- mour ne l'a- ni- me pas?

Oui, mon Dieu, quand mes mains de tout mon héritage Aux pauvres feraient le partage; Quand même pour le nom chrétien, Bravant les croix les plus infâmes, Je livrerais mon corps aux flammes, Si je n'aime, je ne suis rien, Si je n'ai- me, je ne___ suis rien, Si je n'ai- me, je ne suis rien.

Que je vois de Vertus qui bril- lent sur ta tra- ce, Cha- ri- -té, fil- le de la Grâ- ce! A- vec toi mar- che la Dou- -ceur, Que suit, a- vec un air af- fa- ble, La Pa- ti- en- ce in- sé- pa-

-ra- ble De la Paix, son ai- ma- ble sœur, A- vec toi mar- che la Dou-

-ceur, Que suit, a- vec un air af- fa- ble, La Pa- ti- en- ce in- sé- pa-

-ra- ble De la Paix, de la Paix, son ai- ma- ble sœur.

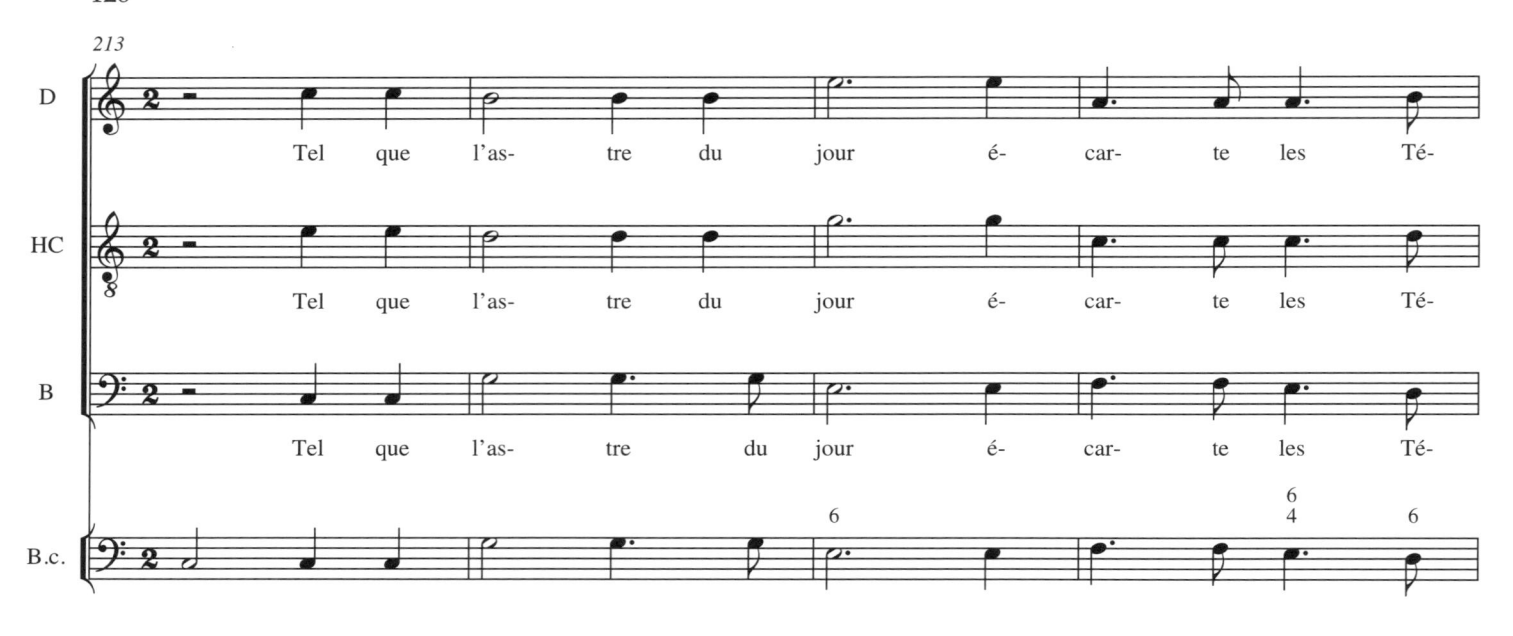

213

D: Tel que l'as- tre du jour é- car- te les Té-
HC: Tel que l'as- tre du jour é- car- te les Té-
B: Tel que l'as- tre du jour é- car- te les Té-
B.c.

217

D: -nè- bres, De la Nuit com- pa- gnes fu- nè- bres, Tel- le tu chas- ses d'un coup
HC: -nè- bres, De la Nuit com- pa- gnes fu- nè- bres, Tel- le tu chas- ses d'un coup
B: -nè- bres, De la Nuit com- pa- gnes fu- nè- bres, Tel- le tu chas- ses d'un coup
B.c.

221

D: d'œil L'en- vie aux hu- mains si fa- ta- le, Et tou- te la trou- pe in- fer-
HC: d'œil L'en- vie aux hu- mains si fa- ta- le, Et tou- te la trou- pe in- fer-
B: d'œil L'en- vie aux hu- mains si fa- ta- le, Et tou- te la trou- pe in- fer-
B.c.

-na- le Des Vi- ces, en- fants de l'or- gueil, Tel- le tu chas- ses d'un coup d'œil L'en- vie aux hu- mains si fa- ta- le, Et tou- te la trou- pe in- fer- na- le Des Vi- ces, en- fants de l'or- gueil.

Li- bre d'am- bi- ti- on, sim- ple, et sans ar- ti- fi- ce, Au-
-tant que tu hais l'in- jus- ti- ce, Au- tant la vé- ri- té te plaît. plaît. Que

129

peut la co- lè- re fa- rou- che Sur un cœur que ja- mais ne tou- che Le soin de son pro- pre in- té- rêt, Que peut la co- lè- re fa- rou- che Sur un cœur que ja- mais ne tou- che Le soin de son pro- pre in- té- rêt?

Aux fai- bles- ses d'au- -trui loin d'ê- tre in- ex- o- ra- ble, Tou- jours d'un voi- le fa- vo- ra- ble Tu t'ef- -for- ces de les cou- vrir. -vrir. Quel tri- om-

284
Vn. 1
Vn. 2
B
- phe man- que à ta gloi- re? L'A- mour sait tout vain- cre, tout croi- re, Tout es- pé-
B.c.
289
Vn. 1
Vn. 2
B
-rer, et tout souf- frir, Quel tri- om- - phe man- que à ta
B.c.
294
Vn. 1
Vn. 2
B
gloi- re? L'A- mour sait tout vain- cre, tout croi- re, Tout es- pé- rer,
B.c.

Un jour Dieu ces- se- ra d'in- spi- rer des o-
et tout souf- frir.
-ra- cles; Le don des lan- gues, les mi- ra- cles, La sci- ence au- ra son dé-
-clin. L'A- mour, la Cha- ri- té di- vi- ne, É- ter- nel- le en son o- ri-
-gi- ne, Ne con- naî- tra ja- mais de fin, L'A- mour, la Cha- ri- té di- vi- ne, É- ter-
-nel- le en son o- ri- gi- ne, Ne con- naî- tra ja- mais de fin.

Nos clartés ici-bas ne sont qu'énigmes sombres;

Mais Dieu, sans voiles et sans ombres, Nous éclairera dans les cieux; cieux; Et ce Soleil inaccessible, Comme à ses yeux je suis vi- si- ble, Se ren- dra vi- si- ble à mes yeux, Et ce So- leil in- ac- ces- si- ble, Com- me à ses yeux je suis vi- -si- ble, Se ren- dra vi- si- ble à mes yeux.

L'A- mour sur tous les

dons l'em- por- te a- vec jus- ti- ce. De no- tre cé- les- te é- di- fi- ce La Foi vi- ve est le fon- de- ment; -ment; La sain- te Es- pé- ran- ce l'é- lè- ve, L'ar- den- te Cha- ri- té l'a- chè- ve Et l'as- su- re é- ter- nel- le- ment, La sain- te Es- pé- ran- ce l'é- lè- ve, L'ar- den- te Cha- ri- té l'a- chè- ve Et l'as- su- re é- ter- nel- le- ment.

Ritournelle

Quand pour-rai- je t'of- frir, ô Cha- ri- té su- prê- me, Au sein de la lu- miè- re *mê- me, Le can- ti- que de mes sou- pirs; Quand pour- -pirs;*

Et tou- jours brû- lant pour ta gloi- re, Tou- jours pui- ser, et tou- jours boi- re Dans la

sour- ce des vrais plai- sirs, Et tou- jours brû- lant pour ta gloi- re, Tou- jours pui-

-ser, et toujours boire Dans la source des vrais plaisirs?

Quand pourrons nous t'offrir, ô Charité suprême,
Quand pourrons nous t'offrir, ô Charité suprême, Au
Quand pourrons nous t'offrir, ô Charité suprême, Au

Au sein de la lumière
sein de la lumière même, Les cantiques de nous sou-
sein de la lumière même, Les cantiques de nous sou-

435
D
même, Les cantiques de nous soupirs; Et toujours brû-
HC
-pirs, Les cantiques de nous soupirs; Et toujours brû-
B
-pirs, Les cantiques de nous soupirs; Et toujours brû-
B.c.
440
D
-lant pour ta gloire, Toujours puiser, et toujours boire, et toujours
HC
-lant pour ta gloire, Toujours puiser, toujours puiser, et toujours
B
-lant pour ta gloire, Toujours puiser, et toujours boi-
B.c.
444
Vn. 1
Vn. 2
D
boire Dans la source des vrais plaisirs,
HC
boire Dans la source des vrais plaisirs,
B
-re Dans la source des vrais plaisirs,
B.c.

140

141

142

Heureux qui, de la sagesse

Jean Racine, *Cantiques spirituels* II

Jean-Noël Marchand

*All basse continue figures in this piece are editorial.

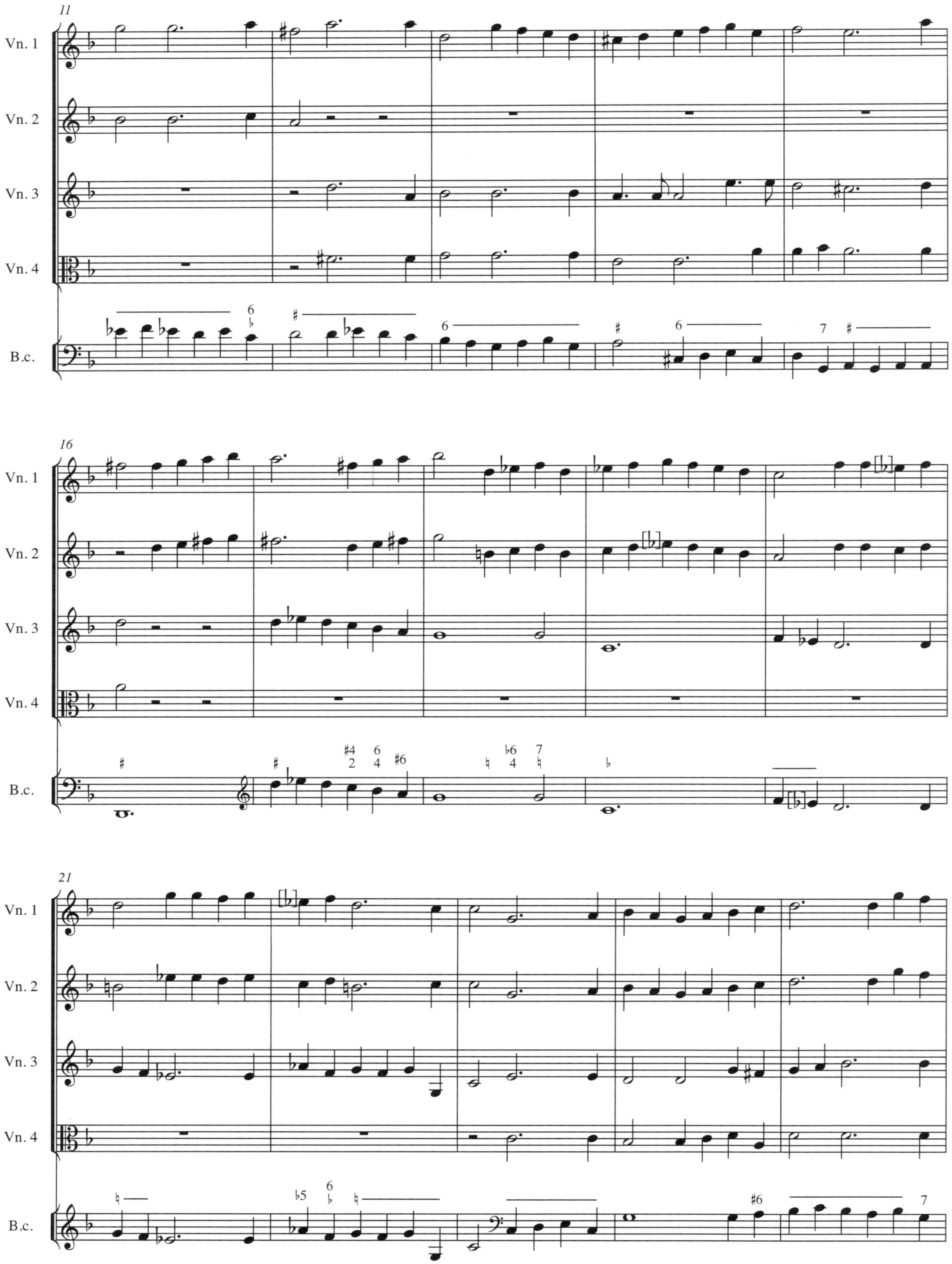
11
Vn. 1
Vn. 2
Vn. 3
Vn. 4
B.c.
16
Vn. 1
Vn. 2
Vn. 3
Vn. 4
B.c.
21
Vn. 1
Vn. 2
Vn. 3
Vn. 4
B.c.

Heu-reux qui, de la sagesse Attendant tout son secours, N'a point mis en la richesse L'espoir de ses derniers jours! Heu-

jours! La mort n'a rien qui l'étonne; Et dès que son Dieu l'ordonne, Son âme prenant l'essor S'élève d'un vol rapide Vers la demeure où réside Son véritable trésor. La

De quelle douleur profonde Seront un jour pénétrés Ces insensés qui du monde, Seigneur, vivent enivrés, De

-vrés, Quand, par u- ne fin sou- dai- ne Dé- trom- pés d'u- ne ombre vai- ne Qui passe et ne re- vient plus, Leurs yeux du fond de l'a- bî- me Près de ton trô- ne su- bli- me Ver- ront bril- ler tes é- lus! Quand,

-lus!

«In- for- tu- nés que nous som- mes, Où s'é- ga-

-raient nos es- prits? Voi- là, di- ront- ils, ces hom- mes, Vils ob- -jets de nos mé- pris. Leur sain- te et pé- ni- ble vi- e Nous pa- -rut u- ne fo- li- e; Mais au- jour- d'hui tri- om- phants, Le ciel chante leur louange Et Dieu lui-même les

range Au nombre de ses enfants, Mais au jour-

-d'hui triomphants, Le ciel chante leur louan-

-ge Et Dieu lui-mê- me les ran- ge Au nom- bre de ses en-

-fants, Et Dieu lui-mê- me les ran- ge Au nom- bre de ses en-

Symphonie

-fants.

Pour trouver un bien fragile Qui nous vient d'être arraché, Par quel chemin difficile Hélas! nous avons marché!

Dans une route insensée
Notre âme en vain s'est lassée,
Sans se reposer jamais, Fermant l'œil à la lumière
Qui nous montrait la carrière

De la bien- heu- reu- se paix.

De nos at- ten- tats in- jus- tes Quel fruit nous est- il res-

-té? Où sont les ti- tres au- gus- tes Dont notre_or- gueil s'est flat- té?

Sans a- mis et sans dé- fen- se, Au trô- ne de la ven- -gean- ce Ap- pe- lés en ju- ge- ment, Fai- bles et tris- tes vic- ti- mes, Nous y ve- nons de nos cri- mes Ac- com- pa- gnés seu- le-

-ment, Fai- bles et tris- tes vic--ti- mes, Nous y ve- nons de nos cri- mes Ac- com- pa- gnés seu- le- ment.»

210
Vn. 1, 2
Vn. 3
Vn. 4
B.c.
1.
2.
215
Symphonie
222
D
HC
B
[Chœur]
Ain- si, d'u- ne
Ain-
[Chœur]
[Chœur]
Ain- si, d'u- ne

voix plain-ti-ve, Ex-pri-me-ra ses re-mords

-si, d'u-ne voix plain-ti-ve, Ex-pri-me-ra ses re-mords

voix plain-ti-ve, Ex-pri-me-ra ses re-mords

La pé-ni-ten-ce tar-di-ve Des in-con-so-la-bles morts.

La pé-ni-ten-ce tar-di-ve Des in-con-so-la-bles morts.

La pé-ni-ten-ce tar-di-ve Des in-con-so-la-bles morts.

[Seule]
Ain- morts. Ce qui fai-sait leurs dé-li-ces, Sei-gneur, fe-

morts.

Ain- morts.

-ra leurs sup- pli- ces;

[Seule]
Et par u- ne é- ga- le loi Tes saints trou- ve- ront des char- mes Dans le sou- ve- nir des lar- mes Qu'ils ver- sent i- ci pour toi.

[Chœur]
Et par une égale loi Tes saints trouveront des charmes Dans le souvenir des larmes Qu'ils versent ici pour

268
Vn. 1, 2
Vn. 3
Vn. 4
D
ver- sent, qu'ils ver- sent i- ci pour toi,
HC
ver- sent, qu'ils ver- sent i- ci pour toi,
B
toi, Qu'ils ver- sent i- ci pour toi,
B.c.
273
Vn. 1, 2
Vn. 3
Vn. 4
D
Et par u- ne é- ga- le loi Tes
HC
Et par u- ne é- ga- le loi Tes
B
Et par u- ne é- ga- le loi Tes
B.c.

saints trouveront des charmes Dans le souvenir des larmes Qu'ils versent ici pour toi, Qu'ils versent i-

-ci _____ pour toi, Qu'ils ver- sent i- ci _____ pour toi.

-ci pour toi, Qu'ils ver- sent i- ci _____ pour toi.

Qu'ils ver- sent, qu'ils ver- sent i- ci pour toi.

Mon Dieu, quelle guerre cruelle!

Jean Racine, *Cantiques spirituels* III

Jean-Noël Marchand

*All basse continue figures in this piece are editorial.

Mon Dieu, quelle guerre cruelle! Je trouve deux hommes en moi; L'un veut que plein d'amour pour toi Mon cœur te soit toujours fidèle. L'autre à tes volontés rebelle Me ré-

-vol- te con- tre ta loi, L'un veut que plein d'a- mour pour toi Mon cœur te soit tou- jours fi- dè- le. L'au- tre à tes vo- lon- tés re- bel- le Me ré- -vol- te con- tre ta loi.

168

-ché. Hé-las! en guer- re a- vec moi- mê- me, Où pour- rai- je trou- ver la paix? Je veux, et n'ac-com- plis ja- mais. Je veux, mais, ô mi- sè- re ex--trê- me! Je ne fais pas le bien que j'ai- me, Et je fais le mal que je hais.

Ô grâce, ô rayon salu- -tai- re, Viens me mettre avec moi d'ac- cord;

Ritournelle

Et domptant par un doux ef-

-fort Cet hom- me qui t'est si con- trai- re, Fais ton es- cla- ve vo- lon- -tai- re De cet es- cla- ve de la mort, Fais ton es- cla- ve vo- lon- tai- re De cet es- -cla- ve de la mort.

Quel charme vainqueur du monde

Jean Racine, *Cantiques spirituels* IV

Jean-Noël Marchand

*All basse continue figures in this piece are editorial.

174

charme vainqueur du monde Vers Dieu m'élève aujourd'hui, Quel charme vainqueur du monde Vers Dieu m'élève aujourd'hui? Malheureux l'homme qui

fonde Sur les hom- mes son ap- pui! Leur gloi- re fuit, et s'ef-
-face En moins de temps que la tra- ce Du vais- seau qui fend les
mers, Ou de la flè- che ra- pi- de Qui loin de l'œil qui la
gui- de Cher- che l'oi- seau dans les airs, Leur gloi- re fuit, et s'ef-
-face En moins de temps que la tra- ce Du vais- seau qui fend les
mers, Ou de la flè- che ra- pi- de Qui loin de l'œil qui la

guí- de Cher- che l'oi- seau dans les airs.

De la Sa- ges- se_im- mor- tel- le La voix ton- ne, et nous in- struit. «En- fants des hom- mes, dit- el- le, De vos soins quel est le fruit? Par quel- le_er- reur, â- mes vai- nes, Du plus pur sang de vos vei- nes A- che- tez- vous si sou- vent, Non un pain qui vous re- pais- se, Mais u- ne_om- bre qui vous lais- se Plus af- fa- més que de- vant?

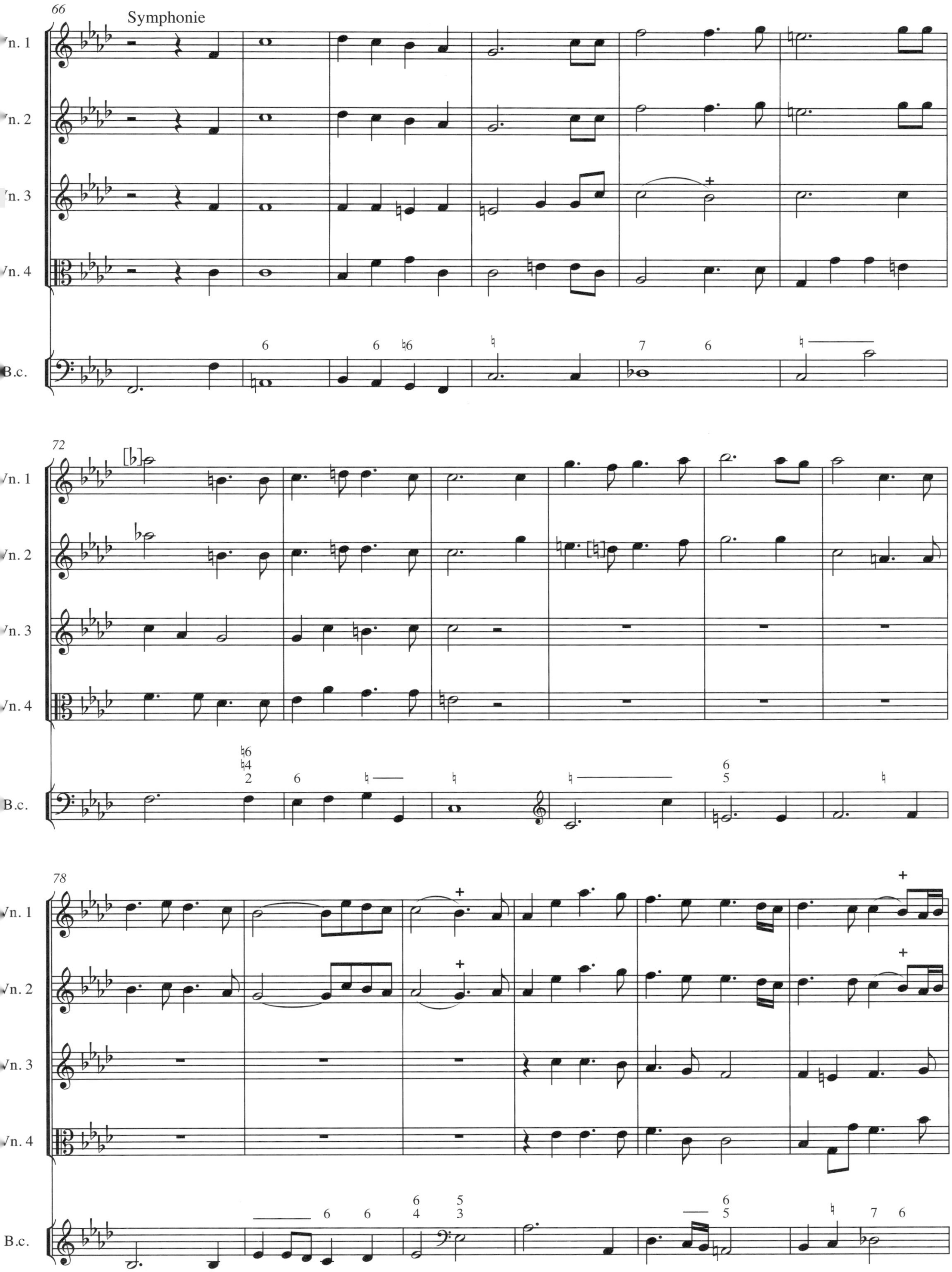
Symphonie
Vn. 1
Vn. 2
Vn. 3
Vn. 4
B.c.

pain que je vous pro- po- se Sert aux An- ges d'a- li- ment; Dieu lui-mê- me le com- po- se De la fleur de son fro- ment. Le

-ment. C'est ce pain si délectable Que ne sert point à sa table Le monde que vous suivez. Je l'offre à qui me veut suivre. Approchez. Voulez-vous vivre? Pre-

Vn. 1, 2
Vn. 3
Vn. 4
D
B.c.
-nez, man- gez, et vi- vez,
Je l'of- fre à qui me veut sui- vre. Ap- pro-
-chez. Vou- lez- vous vi- vre? Pre- nez, man- gez, et vi-

-vez, Ap- pro- chez. Vou- lez- vous vi- vre? Pre- nez, man-

-gez, et vi- vez.»

Ô Sa- ges- se, ta pa- ro- le Fit é-

-clore l'univers, Posa sur un double pôle La terre au milieu des mers. Tu dis, et les cieux parurent, Et tous les astres coururent Dans leur ordre se placer. Avant les siècles tu règnes; Et qui suis-je, que tu daignes Jusqu'à moi te rabaisser, Et qui suis-je, que tu daignes Jusqu'à moi te

183

ra- bais- ser?

Verbe, image du Père, Laissa son trône éternel, Et d'une mortelle mère Voulut naître homme et mortel. Le

-tel. Com- me l'or- gueil fut le cri- me Dont il nais- sait la vic- ti- me, Il dé- pouil-

-la sa splen- deur, Et vint, pau- vre et mi- sé- ra- ble, Ap- pren- dre à l'hom- me cou-

-pa- ble Sa vé- ri- ta- ble gran- deur, Et vint, pau- vre et mi- sé-

-ra- ble, Ap- pren- dre à l'hom- me cou- pa- ble Sa vé- ri- ta- ble gran- deur.

L'â- me heu- reu- se- ment cap- ti- ve Sous ton joug trou- ve la

paix, Et s'a- breu- ve d'une eau vi- ve Qui ne s'é- pui- se ja- mais.

186

Chœur
L'â- me heu- reu- se- ment cap- ti- ve Sous ton joug trou- ve la paix, Et s'a- breu- ve d'u- ne eau

vi- ve Qui ne s'é- pui- se jamais.

vi- ve Qui ne s'é- pui- se jamais.

vi- ve Qui ne s'é- pui- se jamais.

[Seule]
Cha- cun peut boi- re en cet- te on- de; El- le in- vi- te tout

188

boi- re en cet- te on- de, Cha- cun peut boi- re, cha- cun peut boi- re en cet-

Cha- cun peut boi- re, cha- cun peut boi- re, cha- cun peut boi- re en cet-

-de; Cha- cun peut boi- re, cha- cun peut boi- re en cet-

-te on- de; El- le in- vi- te tout le mon- de; [Chœur] Cha- cun peut

-te on- de; El- le in- vi- te tout le mon- de;

-te on- de; El- le in- vi- te tout le mon- de;

243
Vn. 1
Vn. 2
Vn. [3], 4
D
boi- re‿en cet- te‿on- de, Cha- cun peut boi- re, cha- cun peut boi- re, cha- cun peut
[Chœur]
HC
Cha- cun peut boi- re‿en cet- te‿on- de, Cha- cun peut boi- re, cha- cun peut
[Chœur]
B
Cha- cun peut boi- re, cha- cun peut boi- re‿en cet-
B.c.

247
Vn. 1
Vn. 2
Vn. [3], 4
D
boi- re‿en cet- te‿on- de, Cha- cun peut boi- re‿en cet- te‿on- de, Cha- cun peut
HC
boi- re‿en cet- te‿on- de, Cha- cun peut boi- re‿en cet- te‿on- de, Cha- cun peut
B
-te‿on- de; El- le‿in- vi- te tout le mon- de; Cha- cun peut boi- re‿en cet-
B.c.

boi- re, cha- cun peut boi- re en cet- te on- de; El- le in- vi- te tout

-te on- de; Cha- cun peut boi- re en cet- te on- de; El- le in- vi- te tout

le mon- de; Mais nous cou- rons fol- le-

le mon- de; Mais nous cou- rons fol- le- ment, Mais nous cou-

le mon- de; Mais nous cou- rons fol- le- ment

m. 258

D: -ment Cher- cher, cher- cher des sour- ces bour- beu- ses, Mais nous cou-

HC: -rons, Cher- cher des sour- ces bour- beu- ses, Mais nous cou-

B: Cher- cher, cher- cher des sour- ces bour- beu- ses,

m. 261

D: -rons, mais nous cou- rons, Cher- cher des sour- ces bour-

HC: -rons, mais nous cou- rons, Cher- cher des sour- ces bour-

B: Cher- cher, cher- cher, cher- cher des sour- ces bour-

-beu- ses Ou des ci- ter- nes trom- peu- ses D'où l'eau fuit à tout mo-ment, Mais nous cou- rons fol- le- ment, mais nous cou- rons, mais nous cou-

194

Settings of Individual
Cantiques spirituels

Heureux qui, de la sagesse

Premier Verset

Jean Racine, *Cantiques spirituels* II

Duhalle

Second Verset

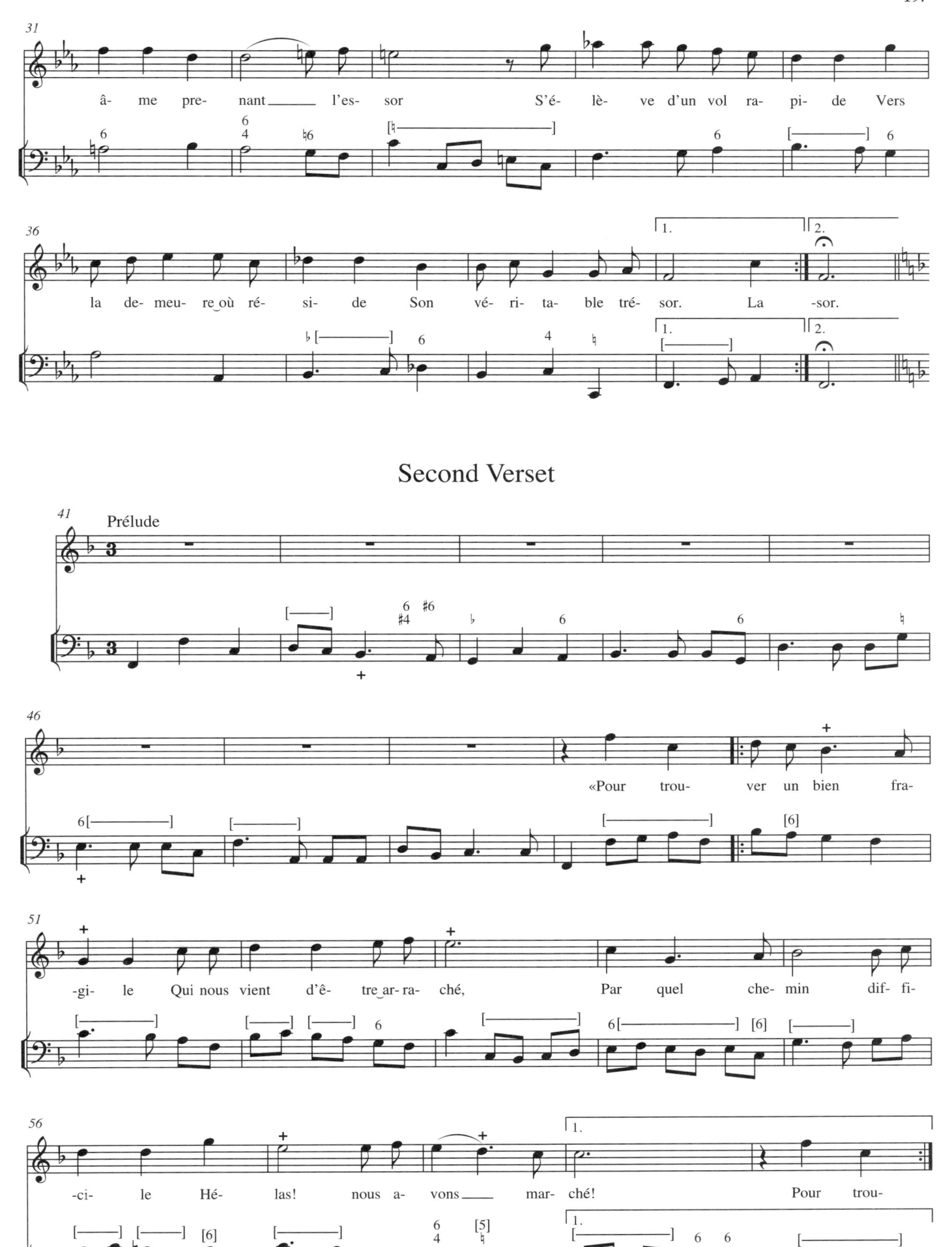

Prélude

«Pour trouver un bien fragile Qui nous vient d'être arraché, Par quel chemin difficile Hélas! nous avons marché! Pour trou-

-ché! Dans une route insensée Notre âme en vain s'est lassée, Sans se reposer jamais, Fermant l'œil à la lumière Qui nous montrait la carrière De la bienheureuse paix. paix.»

Troisième Verset

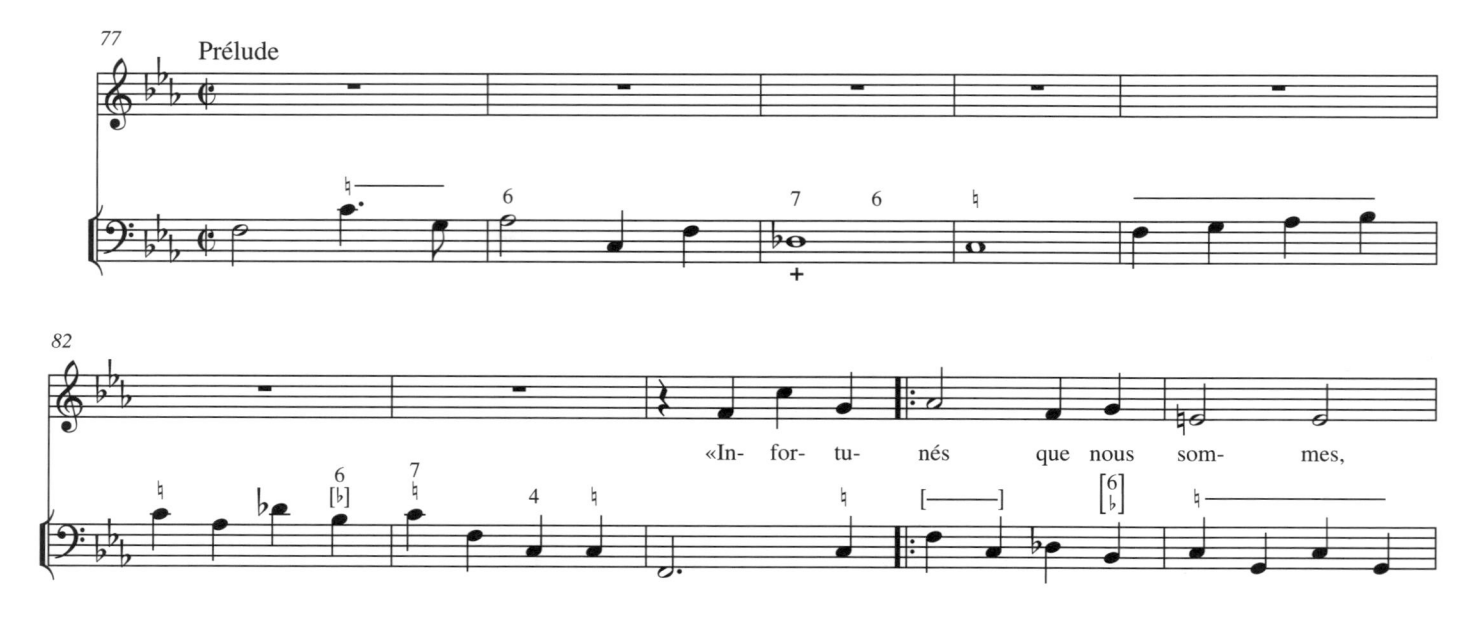

Prélude

«Infortunés que nous sommes,

Où s'é- ga- raient nos es- prits? Voi- là, di- ront- ils, ces hom- mes, Vils ob- -jets de nos mé- pris. In- for- tu- -pris. Leur sain- te et pé- ni- ble vi- e Nous pa- rut u- ne fo- li- e; Mais au- jour- d'hui tri- om- phants, Le ciel chan- te leur lou- an- ge Et Dieu lui- mê- me les ran- ge Au nom- bre de ses en- fants. Leur -fants.»

Quatrième Verset

Prélude

De quelle douleur pro-fonde Seront un jour pénétrés Ces insensés qui du monde, Seigneur, vivent enivrés, Devrés, Quand, par une fin soudaine Détrompés d'une ombre vaine Qui passe et ne revient plus, Leurs yeux du fond de l'abîme Près de ton

201

trô- ne su- bli- me Ver- ront bril- ler tes é- lus! -lus!

Cinquième Verset

[Prélude]

«De nos at- ten- tats in- -jus- tes Quel fruit nous est- il res- té? Où sont les ti- tres au- -gus- tes Dont notre orgueil s'est flat- té? -té? Sans a- -mis et sans dé- fen- se, Au trô- ne de la ven- gean- ce Ap- pe-

-lés en jugement, Faibles et tristes victimes, Nous y venons de nos crimes Accompagnés seulement. Sans a- -ment.»

Dernier Verset du Cantique de Monsieur Racine

[Prélude]

Ainsi, d'une voix plaintive, Exprimera ses remords La pénitence tardive Des inconsolables morts. Ain-

morts. Ce qui fai- sait leurs dé- li- ces, Sei- gneur, fe- ra leurs sup-

-pli- ces; Et par u- ne é- ga- le loi Tes

saints trou- ve- ront des char- mes Dans le sou- ve- nir des

lar- mes Qu'ils ver- sent i- ci pour toi. Ce qui fai- toi.

Mon Dieu, quelle guerre cruelle!

Jean Racine, *Cantiques spirituels* III

Duhalle

Suite du Cantique

L'un tout es--prit, et tout cé- les- te, Veut qu'au ciel sans ces- se a- ta- ché, Et des biens é- ter- nels tou- ché, Je com- pte pour rien tout le res- te; Et l'au- tre par son poids fu- nes- te Me tient vers la ter- re pen- ché.

Suite du Cantique

Hé- las! en guer- re a- vec moi-

-mê- me, Où pour- rai- je trou- ver la paix? Hé- paix? Je veux, et n'ac- com- plis ja- mais. Je veux, mais, ô mi- sè- re ex- trê- me! Je ne fais pas le bien que j'ai- me, Et je fais le mal que je hais. Je hais.

Fin du Cantique

Prélude

Ô

grâce, ô ray- on sa- lu- tai- re, Viens me met- tre a- vec moi d'ac-
-cord; Ô -cord; Et dom- ptant par un doux ef- fort Cet
hom- me qui t'est si con- trai- re, Fais ton es- cla- ve vo- lon-
-tai- re De cet es- cla- ve de la mort. Et dom- mort.

Hélas! en guerre avec moi-même

Jean Racine, *Cantiques spirituels* III.3

Jean-Baptiste de Bousset

Hé-las! en guer-re a-vec moi-mê- me, Où pour-rai- je, où pour-rai- je trou--ver la paix? Je veux, je veux, et n'ac-com-plis ja--mais. Je veux, mais, ô mi-sè- re ex-trê- me! Je ne fais pas le bien que j'ai- me, Et je fais le mal que je hais, Et je fais le mal que je hais, Je ne fais pas le bien que j'ai- me, Et je fais le mal que je hais. Je hais.

Critical Report

Library Sigla

F-Pn   Paris, Bibliothèque nationale de France

F-Psg   Paris, Bibliothèque Sainte-Geneviève

F-V   Versailles, Bibliothèque municipale

GB-Lbl   London, The British Library

PL-Kc   Kraków, Muzeum Narodowe, Biblioteka XX Czartoryskich

US-Cn   Chicago, Newberry Library

Sources

Moreau and Lalande's settings of Racine's *Cantiques spirituels* are transcribed from the first printed edition of 1695:

CANTIQUES | CHANTEZ | DEVANT LE ROY, | ET COMPOSEZ | Par Monsieur MOREAU, Maistre de Musique. | & Pensionnaire de Sa Majesté. | PROPRES POUR LES DAMES RELIGIEUSES, | & toutes autres personnes. | A PARIS, | Chez Cristophe Ballard, seul Imprimeur du Roy | pour la Musique, ruë S. Jean de Beauvais, | au Mont Parnasse | M. DC. XCV. | Avec Privilege de Sa Majesté.

Moreau's three settings occupy pages 2–17 (*Les méchants m'ont vanté*), 18–24 (*Mon Dieu, quelle guerre cruelle!*), and 25–37 (*Quel charme vainqueur du monde*). Lalande's setting of Racine's second cantique, *Heureux qui, de la sagesse,* appears last in the print, on pages 38–57. Interspersed with the Lalande setting are alternative duo versions of the final reprises of the third and fourth stanzas (pp. 46–47 and 50–51, respectively) and of the entire fifth stanza (pp. 54–55); transcriptions of these sections are given in the appendix of this edition.

Four copies of Moreau and Lalande's print survive in F-Pn under the shelfmarks Vm1 1168, D. 8284, Rés. 855, and X. 1089. The latter three include alternative versions of four individual stanzas, handwritten at the end of the volume: two from Moreau's setting of *Les méchants m'ont vanté* ("Que je vois de Vertus" for two voices and "L'Amour sur tous les dons" for three voices) and two from Moreau's setting of *Mon Dieu, quelle guerre cruelle!* ("L'un tout esprit, et tout céleste" and "Ô grâce, ô rayon salutaire," both for two voices). D. 8284 was used for the transcription of these stanzas, which appear in the appendix of this edition. In this source, the alternative setting of "Que je vois de Vertus" is given on a formerly blank page later hand-numbered 1; "L'Amour sur tous les dons" on a page hand-numbered 4; "L'un tout esprit, et tout céleste" on hand-numbered pages 1–2; and "Ô grâce, ô rayon salutaire" on hand-numbered pages 2–3. According to Thierry Favier, all three copies are apparently in the same hand.[1]

The 1695 print is the earliest known source of the settings by Moreau and Lalande and is no doubt the basis used for the following handwritten copies of the work: F-Pn, Rés. 1652 and Vm7 3424; F-V, MS mus 51 and 54; and US-Cn, Case MS VM 1510.M88a. One of the copies in F-Pn, Vm7 3424, includes a number of changes and errors, and it prefaces Moreau's first cantique with the instrumental introduction from Marchand's setting of the same text; because of its general unreliability, and because of its unclear relationship to the composer, this source has not been consulted for the edition. Unfortunately, neither the prints nor the manuscript copies include instrumental parts other than the basse continue, even though the preface ("Au lecteur") specifically mentions them.[2]

A second edition of Moreau and Lalande's collection appeared in 1699, made from the same plates as the first, but featuring a new foreword:

CANTIQUES | CHANTEZ | DEVANT LE ROY, | PROPRES POUR LES DAMES RELIGIEUSES, | et toutes autres personnes; | Par Monsieur Moreau, Maître de Musique, et Pensionnaire de Sa Majesté. | NOUVELLE EDITION, DE L'IMPRIMERIE | De J.B. CHRISTOPHE BALLARD, seul Imprimeur du Roy pour la Musique. | A Paris | rüe Saint Jean de Beauvais, au Mont-Parnasse. | M. DCC. XIX. | Avec Privilège de Sa Majesté.

In addition to a copy in F-Pn (Mus. 863), the 1699 print survives integrated into the *Recueil d'airs spirituels, cantiques, et noëls de différents auteurs, tome II* (Paris: Christophe Ballard, 1728) in GB-Lbl, K.7.c.8 and PL-Kc, 2994 ew.1.

The works by Collasse are transcribed from the following print, also published by Christophe Ballard in 1695:

CANTIQUES | SPIRITUELS, | MIS | EN MUSIQUE | Par P. COLLASSE, Maistre de la Musique | de la Chapelle du Roy. | A PARIS, | Par Cristophe Ballard, seul Imprimeur du Roy | pour la Musique, ruë S. Jean de Beauvais, | au Mont Parnasse. | M. DC. XCV. | Avec Privilegé de Sa Majesté.

Collasse's setting of Racine's first cantique, *Les méchants m'ont vanté*, occupies pages 1–47 of the print; the second, *Heureux qui, de la sagesse*, occupies pages 49–80;

the third, *Mon Dieu, quelle guerre cruelle!*, pages 81–96; and the fourth, *Quel charme vainqueur du monde*, pages 97–137.

The two surviving copies of the Collasse print can be found in F-Pn, Vm1 1624 and MUS 864. One manuscript copy based on the print survives as well: F-Pn, Rés. F 440, in which the transverse flute (*flûte allemande*) is replaced by recorder (*flûte*).

Marchand's settings of Racine's *Cantiques spirituels* survive in a single manuscript copy in F-Pn, manuscript Rés. 1262:

CANTIQUES | SPIRITUELS | FAITS PAR M RACINE POUR ESTRE MIS EN | MUSIQUE | ET | Mis en Musique Par Marchand l'aisné | Ordinaire de la Musique de la chapelle et chambre | Du Roy | Et organiste de l'eglise Royalle de Nostre Dame de Versailles

The manuscript is available in a facsimile edition edited by Thierry Favier (Courlay, France: Editions J. M. Fuzeau, 1999). Marchand's first setting, *Les méchants m'ont vanté*, occupies pages 1–26 of the manuscript; the second, *Heureux qui, de la sagesse,* pages 27–49; the third, *Mon Dieu, quelle guerre cruelle!*, pages 51–59; and the fourth, *Quel charme vainqueur du monde,* pages 61–79.

Duhalle's two *Cantiques de M. Racine* and Jean-Baptiste de Bousset's air "Hélas! en guerre avec moi-même" are taken respectively from the following anthologies printed by Christophe Ballard:

PSEAUMES | ET | CANTIQUES | SPIRITUELS, | MIS | EN MUSIQUE | AVEC LA BASSE-CONTINUE. | PAR MONSIEUR ***** | A PARIS, | Chez CRISTOPHE BALLARD, seul Imprimeur du Roy | pour la Musique, ruë Saint Jean de Beauvais, | au Mont Parnasse. | M. DC. XCV. | Avec Privilege de Sa Majesté.

AIRS | SPIRITUELS | DES MEILLEURS AUTHEURS. | Livre second. | A PARIS, | Chez CRISTOPHE BALLARD, seul Imprimeur du Roy pour la Musique, | ruë S. Jean de Beauvais, au Mont-Parnasse. | M. DCCI. | Avec Privilege de Sa Majesté.

The only surviving copy of the *Pseaumes et cantiques spirituels* is in F-Psg, Vm 22 RES. Duhalle's two cantiques appear repsectively on pages 38–49 (*Heureux qui, de la sagesse*) and 90–93 (*Mon Dieu, quelle guerre cruelle!*) of the anthology. Copies of the 1701 *Airs spirituels* survive in F-Pn, Rés. 229 bis and Vm1 1572, and in PL-Kc, 2994 ew.1 as part of the *Recueil d'airs spirituels* (1728). Bousset's air occupies pages 76–77 of *Airs spirituels des meilleurs autheurs*.

Editorial Methods

The works in the edition are ordered as follows: large-scale settings of all four of Racine's cantiques by Moreau, Lalande, Collasse, and Marchand are given first, in chronological order, followed by the smaller-scale settings of individual poems or stanzas by Duhalle and Bousset. Within these groupings, the ordering of the works in the original sources has been preserved. Titles used in this edition are editorial and are based on the text incipits of Racine's poetry; the full descriptive titles from the original sources are given in the critical notes. Text credits have been added at the beginning of each piece to clarify the numbering of the Racine texts, since this does not always correspond to the numbering of the musical settings within the sources. All textual elements, including tempo markings, section labels (Ritournelle, Récit, Chœur, etc.), designations of vocal and instrumental parts, and written instructions have been standardized, regardless of how they appear in the sources, and their placement and alignment have been regularized. Any textual elements in brackets have been added editorially.

The original designations of vocal and instrumental parts, where given, are retained. Added designations are shown in brackets. Modern score order has been adopted (vocal parts often appear above string parts in the sources), and flute and violin parts in the Collasse settings, which share staves in the original, are given their own staves.

Two passages in Collasse's setting of *Quel charme vainqueur du monde* (mm. 32–59, 85–113) feature a violin (usually Violon 2) as the lowest part of the texture, with the basse continue line resting. In the edition, the music of the second violin part has been placed in the basse continue part in cue-size notation (without figures, as in the source) for the benefit of modern performers who wish to double this line. In measure 251 of the same setting, the lowest line of the source is marked "B.C. 2. Violon," indicating that it is to be played by both Violon 2 and the basse continue; thus, in the edition, this line is given in full-size notation in both parts. For each of these cases, the source directive indicating the instrumental change is given in the critical notes.

All instrumental and vocal parts originally in G1, G2, or C1 clefs are transcribed in treble clef. Parts originally in C5 or F4 clefs are transcribed in bass clef; parts originally in F3 clef are transcribed in either bass clef or transposed treble clef as appropriate. In the settings by Marchand, the Violon 4 part in C2 clef is transcribed in alto clef (for viola), and the Haute-contre part in C3 clef is transcribed in transposed treble clef (for tenor). Original cleffings are specified in incipits at the beginning of each setting. The time signatures of the original sources have been retained: a signature of **3** is generally equivalent to $\frac{3}{4}$, and both **2** and ¢ are used to indicate a duple meter with two half notes (or equivalent) per measure.

The note and rest values of the sources have been transcribed in a 1:1 ratio, with some tacit adjustments to the visual presentation of rests. Other adjustments to source rhythmic values are discussed on a case-by-case basis in the critical notes. Editorially added notes and rests appear in brackets.

The notation of repeats and subsequent endings in the sources—often inconsistent or ambiguous—has been regularized throughout the edition to conform to modern practice. Occasionally it has been necessary, for purposes of clarification, to add open repeats to beginnings of repeated sections, to insert extra measures into first endings, or to adjust the final note values of subsequent endings; these emendations have been made without further indication in the critical notes. The barring of the sources is generally consistent with modern practice and has been retained in the edition; double barlines are retained or added at the ends of stanzas or other major sections.

The original sign ♯ is transcribed as ♯ or ♮ depending on context (as is ♭ when it is used to mean ♮), with no further indication in the critical notes. All accidentals that appear in the original are retained in the edition, even if redundant, and are assumed to apply for the remainder of the measure, per modern practice. Any accidentals on the staff that appear in brackets have been added by the editor. Brackets are also used when a repetition of the same pitch extends over a barline in the transcription and only the first note in the series has an accidental in the original. In cases where an editorial accidental precedes the first inflection of the same pitch in the source, both accidentals are given in the edition. If an original or bracketed accidental on the staff is no longer valid when the same pitch is repeated later in the same measure, it is canceled with a bracketed natural sign when the source does not indicate cancellation. Cautionary accidentals are not normally supplied. Accidentals inferred from or required by the figured bass are supplied by the editor in brackets.

Text underlay in the sources is generally straightforward and has been maintained in the edition. The spelling and punctuation of the cantique texts have been modernized to conform to the most recent edition of the poems by Jean Racine (*Cantiques spirituels et autres poèmes*, ed. Jean-Pierre Lemaire [Paris: Éditions Gallimard, 1999]). Text credits use roman numerals to refer to the ordering of each cantique within its original literary publication (*Cantiques spirituels faits par Monsieur R. . . . pour estre mis en musique* [Paris: Denys Thierry, 1695]), with stanza numbers specified in arabic numerals as necessary; thus "*Cantiques spirituels* II" refers to Racine's second cantique (*Heureux qui, de la sagesse*), and "*Cantiques spirituels* III.3" refers to the third stanza ("Hélas! en guerre avec moi-même") of Racine's third cantique (*Mon Dieu, quelle guerre cruelle!*). First letters of poetic lines have been capitalized regardless of their appearance in the musical sources. Where text is repeated, however, this capitalization is maintained only for the repetition of entire poetic lines; commas are added where needed to clarify text repetition. Word division follows modern French practice. Added text is placed in brackets.

Slurs used in the sources to indicate melismas in the vocal parts are inconsistent and have been tacitly replaced by modern slurring and beaming; slurs have not been applied in a few longer melismatic passages. Beaming and slurring in the instrumental parts is likewise inconsistent in the sources and has been adapted to conform to modern practice. Stem directions have been modernized throughout.

The principal ornament sign used in this era of French music is a cross symbol (+) to indicate a trill. In a few cases, the printer has used a different sign (⁓ or *t*) for the same ornament; these have been tacitly changed to the cross symbol. Trills in all parts except the basse continue are placed above the notes to which they apply, regardless of where they occur in the sources. Trills in the basse continue part are placed below their notes. Various note values are used to notate appoggiaturas in the sources, although it is unknown whether or not this signifies any difference in execution; the original values have been retained in this edition.

All basse continue figures are noted above the staff, regardless of where they appear in the source, and are placed metrically to correspond to the indicated harmonic changes. Figures are stacked from lowest to highest to conform with modern practice. The original figuring of the source has been retained with one exception: when inflections to figures are indicated by a separate symbol, the inflection is placed before the figure (e.g., ♯6, rather than 6♯). Sharps and flats used as figures are modernized as natural signs when appropriate. Editorially added figures are supplied in square brackets, except in the Marchand settings; all figures in these settings are editorial, since no figures are present in the original manuscript source. The continuo parts for the four alternative verses in the appendix are absent in the original; for the edition, they were adapted from the 1695 edition of Moreau's *Cantiques chantez devant le Roy*, with changes indicated in the critical notes. In the printed sources of the works by Moreau, Lalande, Collasse, and Duhalle, slur-like markings are used to denote the extension of a figure over more than one note; where necessary, these have been tacitly replaced with straight extender lines following modern practice.

Critical Notes

The notes below include the title of each piece as given in the source, additional comments on textual variations (where necessary), and rejected source readings that are not otherwise covered in the editorial methods. Locations within each setting are identified by measure number (M., Mm.) and part. Notes are numbered consecutively within each measure, with appoggiaturas included in the count. The following abbreviations for instrumental and vocal parts are used: Fl. = Flûte/Flûte allemande, Vn. = Violon, D = Dessus, HC = Haute-contre, B = Basse, B.c. = Basse continue. Pitches are identified according to the system in which middle C is c′.

Moreau and Lalande, "Cantiques chantez devant le Roy"

LES MÉCHANTS M'ONT VANTÉ (MOREAU)

Title. CANTIQUE PREMIER | A LA LOUANGE DE LA CHARITÉ. | Tiré de S. Paul 1. aux Corinthiens Chap. 13.

Notes. M. 40, D, note 1 is dotted quarter. M. 58, B.c., note 1 is half tied to quarter. M. 59, B.c., note 1 is half tied to quarter. Mm. 90–109, D, clef is C1; B.c., clef is C3. Mm. 151–71, D, clef is C1; B.c., clef is C1. M. 183, B.c., note 2, figure is 7. M. 203, B.c., note 1 is half tied to quarter. M. 207, D, notes 1–2 are dotted half.

MON DIEU, QUELLE GUERRE CRUELLE! (MOREAU)

Title. CANTIQUE SECOND. | Plainte d'un Chrestien, sur les contrarietez qu'il éprouve | au dedans de luy-mesme. | Tirée de S. Paul aux Rom. Chap. 7.

Notes. M. 8, B.c., through m. 13, note 1, clef is C3. M. 19, no repeat sign. M. 29, D, B.c., note is whole. Mm. 53, B.c., note 2 through m. 56, note 1, clef is C3.

Quel charme vainqueur du monde (Moreau)

Title. CANTIQUE TROISIÈME. | SUR LES VAINES OCCUPATIONS | des gens du Siecle | Tiré de divers endroits d'Isaïe et de Jeremie.

Notes. M. 30, B.c., note is 8th followed by 8th rest. M. 52, D has "Chœur." M. 65, D, note 7 is c♯". M. 67, B.c., note 1 is c♯. M. 98, B.c., note 3, figure is 6. M. 107, B.c., note 1 is whole. M. 126, B.c., note is half tied to half. M. 133, "Seul, et chœur en suite" moved from m. 130.

Heureux qui, de la sagesse (Lalande)

Title. CANTIQUE QUATRIÈME. | SUR LE BONHEUR DE JUSTES, | & sur le malheur des Reprouvez. | Tiré de la Sagesse, Chap. 5.

Notes. M. 53, repeat sign is missing. M. 78, meter is **2**. M. 143, B.c., note 2, figure is $^{5\flat}_{6}$. Mm. 168, repeat sign moved from m. 167. M. 170, repeat sign is missing. M. 172, D2, note 4 through m. 173, note 2, text is "leur supplice."

Collasse, "Cantiques spirituels, mis en musique"

Les méchants m'ont vanté

Title. CANTIQUE PREMIER | A LA LOUANGE DE LA CHARITÉ. | Tiré de S. Paul 1. aux Corinthiens Chap. 13.

Notes. M. 6, B.c., note 1, figure is 5♭. M. 7, B.c., note 2, figure is 5♭. M. 10, B.c., note 2, figure is $^{6}_{♯4}$. M. 24, B.c., slur spans notes 3–4. M. 28, B.c., note 3, figure is $^{7}_{4}$. M. 48, B.c., note 3, figure is 3. M. 128, B.c., note 4, figure is ♯6. M. 135, B.c., note 3 has figure ♮5. M. 151, B.c., beat 1, figure is $^{6}_{8}$. M. 193, D1, notes 2–3 are 16th–16th. M. 212, B.c., note 1 is G. M. 246, B.c., note 3, figure is 3. Mm. 248–75, B.c., clef is C1. M. 252, B.c., note 4, figure is 6. M. 258, B.c., note 4, figure is 6. M. 261, B.c., note 4, figure is $^{6}_{♯4}$. M. 262, D1 has "Récit." M. 264, B.c., note 5, figure is $^{6}_{♯4}$. M. 269, B.c., note 5, figure is $^{6}_{♯4}$. M. 270, Fl. 1, note 1 is half; rest 1 is missing. M. 274, Fl. 2, note 1, ornament is missing. M. 292, B.c., beat 3, figure is 3. M. 325, B.c., note 4, figure is 3. M. 371, B.c., beat 2, figure is $^{4}_{3}$. M. 402, B.c., note 1 is b. M. 419, B.c., note 1, figure is 5♭. M. 437, D3, note 3 is f'.

Heureux qui, de la sagesse

Title. CANTIQUE SECOND | SUR LE BONHEUR DES JUSTES, | & sur le malheur des Reprouvez. | Tiré de la Sagesse Chap. 5.

Notes. M. 29, B.c., figure is ♮. M. 30, B.c., figure is ♮. M. 55, D1, notes 1–6 are all 32nds. M. 58, B.c., note 2, figure is 6♯. Mm. 88–124, B.c., clef is C2. M. 101, D1 has "Recit." M. 104, B.c., note 2, figure is $^{6}_{5}$. M. 114, B.c., note 3, figure is 3. M. 122, B.c., beat 3, figure is $^{7}_{5♯}$. M. 127, B.c., extender line between notes 1 and 2. M. 143, B.c., extender line between notes 1 and 2. M. 155, D1 has "Reprise." M. 194, B.c., note 3, figure is 3. M. 203, B.c., note 2 through m. 264, clef is C2. M. 209, D2, note 3 is e'; B.c., note 2, figure is ♯6. M. 211, D3, notes 4–5 are tied. M. 220, D3, notes 4–5 are tied. M. 230, B.c., note 1, figure is 6.

Mon Dieu, quelle guerre cruelle!

Title. CANTIQUE TROISIÈME. | OU | Plainte d'un Chrestien, | sur les contrarietez qu'il éprouve au dedans | de luy-mesme. | Tiré de S. Paul aux Romains, Chap. 7.

Notes. M. 18, B.c., note 5 is quarter. M. 25, B.c., note 1 is dotted quarter. M. 29, B.c., note 4, figure is 3. M. 63, D1, note 4 is g'. M. 83, B.c., note 1, figure is 3. M. 94, B.c., note 2 through m. 140, clef is C2. M. 99, B.c., erroneous C1 clef. M. 109, B.c., note 1 has figure 5. M. 111, B.c., note 1 is g'. M. 129, D3, beat 2 is dotted 8th–16th. M. 134, D2, note 2 is b'. M. 135, D2, note 2 is a'. M. 136, D1, note 2 is 8th note and 8th rest.

Quel charme vainqueur du monde

Title. CANTIQUE QUATRIÈME, | Sur les vaines occupations des gens du Siecle. | Tiré de divers endroits d'Isaïe, et de Jeremie.

Notes. M. 32, Vn. 1, note 2, part is marked "Premier Violon seul"; Vn. 2, note 2, part is marked "Second Violon seul." M. 58, D1, notes 2–3 are 16th–16th. M. 76, B.c., note 1, figure is 6. M. 85, Vn. 2, note 2, part is marked "Violon." M. 89, D1, note 1 is b'. M. 95, Vn. 2, part is marked "B.C. Violon." M. 121, Fl. 2, Vn. 2, note 4, trill moved from note 5. M. 136, B.c., note 1 is d♯. M. 139, Vn. 1, beat 3, part is marked "Violon seul"; Vn. 2, beat 3, part is marked "Violon seul." M. 144, D2, note 1 is a'. M. 148, B.c., note 1, figure is $^{4}_{♯6}$. M. 171, B.c., note 1 through m. 221, note 1, clef is C2. M. 193, B.c., note 1, figure is $^{7}_{}$. Mm. 214, B.c., erroneous C1 clef. M. 227, B.c., note 1 is d♯. M. 228, B.c., note 1 is g♯. M. 251, Vn. 2, part is marked "B.C. 2. Violon." M. 298, D2 has "Recit." M. 323, B.c., note 1, figure is ♭. M. 333, B.c., note 1, figure is ♭6.

Marchand, "Cantiques spirituels faits par M Racine"

Les méchants m'ont vanté

Title. Cantique I | a la loüange de la Charité | tiré de S^t. Paul I. aux corinthiens chap. 13.

Comment. In the three-voice statements of the final stanza of the poem, the text is rendered in the first-person plural instead of singular. Thus, in mm. 425–26, "Quand pourrai-je" becomes "Quand pourrons-nous," and in mm. 433–36 "de mes soupirs" becomes "de nos soupirs."

Notes. M. 44, open repeat sign moved from m. 43. M. 80, open repeat sign moved from m. 79. M. 100, repeat sign is missing. M. 441–47, Vn. 1, Vn. 2, erroneous G2 clefs.

HEUREUX QUI, DE LA SAGESSE

Title. [title page] CANTIQUE | SECOND | SUR LE BONHEUR DES IUSTES | ET | Sur le Malheur des Reprouvez | tiré de la Sagesse Chapitre 5.

[above music] Cantique Second. Sur le bonheur | Des justes, et sur le malheur des Réprouvez | tiré de la Sagesse chap. 5ᵉ.

Notes. M. 49, B.c., note is whole. M. 50, Vn. 4, notes 1–2 are half–half. M. 86, Vn. 1 is dotted half note followed by quarter rest. M. 88, Vn. 3, note is half. M. 89, meter is **2**. Mm. 121–28, Vn. 1, erroneous G2 clef. M. 185, B.c., note 1 is half tied to quarter. M. 227, repeat sign is missing. M. 291, D, note 3 is 8th. M. 292, repeat sign.

MON DIEU, QUELLE GUERRE CRUELLE!

Title. [title page] CANTIQUE | TROISIEME | OU PLAINTE DUN CHRESTIEN | Sur les Contrarietez qu'il éprouve au dedans de luy mesme | tiré de Sᵗ. Paul aux Rom. chap. 7.

[above music] 3ᵉ Cantique | Plainte d'un chrestien, sur les contrarietez qu'il éprouve au dedans de luy mesme | tiré de Sᵗ. Paul. aux Rom. ch. 7.

Notes. M. 76, Vn. 1, Vn. 2, B, phrasing mark (vertical stroke) after note 1. M. 78, Vn. 1, Vn. 2, B, phrasing mark after note 1 and note 2. M. 118, repeat sign.

QUEL CHARME VAINQUEUR DU MONDE

Title. Cantique 4ᵉ | Sur les Vaines occupations des gens du siecle | tiré de divers endroits de Jeremie, d'Isaïe

Notes. M. 28, B.c., note is quarter tied to half. M. 31, B.c., note 1 is half tied to dotted 8th tied to 16th. M. 56, B, phrasing mark (vertical stroke) after note 1. M. 62, B, phrasing mark after note 2. M. 63, B, phrasing mark after note 2. M. 121, Vn. 4, note 1 is dotted half. M. 136, repeat sign. M. 138, HC, phrasing mark after note 2. M. 179, D, phrasing mark after note 1. M. 185, D, phrasing mark after note 1. M. 203, HC, notes 4–5, slur moved from notes 3–4. M. 211, D, note 1 is 8th; note 2 is full size (not appoggiatura). M. 239, Vn. 2, note 2 is missing. M. 263, Vn. 1, note 1 is g″. M. 264, meter is **2**. M. 268, meter is ₵; HC, note 1 is a♯. M. 273, D, note 3 is g′. M. 274, HC, notes 1–2 are e′–e′. M. 277, repeat sign.

Duhalle, "Heureux qui, de la sagesse"

Title. Cantique de Monsieur Racine, Premier Verset.

Comment. This setting changes the order of the stanzas from the original poem to 1, 4, 3, 2, 5, 6. The B.c. part is labeled "Basse Continue de M. L. B."

Notes. M. 4, B.c., note 2 through m. 8, note 4, clef is C3. M. 65, B.c., notes 1–2 are slurred. M. 94, D, note 3 is a′. M. 111, B.c., note 4, figure is 3. M. 125, B.c., note 3, figure is 5♭. M. 133, D, note 3 is 16th. M. 172, B.c., note 3, figure is $^6_5$. Mm. 184–87, B.c., clef is C1.

Duhalle, "Mon Dieu, quelle guerre cruelle!"

Title. Cantique de Monsieur Racine.

Comment. The B.c part is labeled "Basse Continue de M. L. B."

Notes. M. 2, B.c., note 1, figure is ♯6. M. 6, B.c., notes are slurred. M. 7, B.c., notes 2–3 are slurred. M. 22, note 3 through m. 23, note 1, D, text is "rebelle." M. 22, B.c., note 1, figure is ♮5. M. 29, D, B.c., note is whole. M. 76, B.c., notes are slurred. M. 78, D, B.c., note is whole.

Bousset, "Hélas! en guerre avec moi-même"

Note. M. 30, D, B.c., "Fin."

Notes

1. Thierry Favier, "Les Cantiques spirituels de Racine mis en musique: aspects esthétiques d'un succès programmé," *La Licorne* 50 (1999): 116.

2. See "Jean Racine's *Cantiques spirituels*" and "The Music" in the introduction.

Appendix

Alternative Settings by Moreau and Lalande of Individual Stanzas

Que je vois de Vertus

Stanza 6 of *Les méchants m'ont vanté* (mm. 69–89)

Jean Racine, *Cantiques spirituels* I.6
Jean-Baptiste Moreau

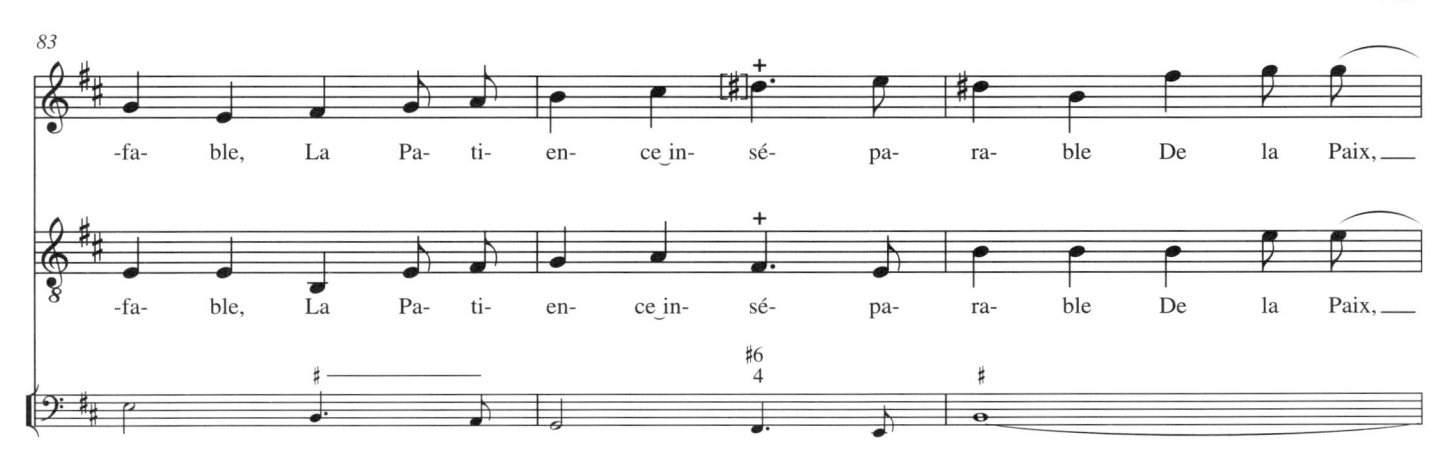

L'Amour sur tous les dons

Stanza 12 of *Les méchants m'ont vanté* (mm. 172–87)

Jean Racine, *Cantiques spirituels* I.12

Jean-Baptiste Moreau

-ce. De no- tre cé- les- te é- di- fi- ce

-ce. De no- tre cé- les- te é- di- fi- ce

-ce. De no- tre cé- les- te é- di- fi- ce La Foi vi- ve est le fon- de-

L'ar- den- te Cha- ri- té l'a-

La sain- te Es- pé- ran- ce l'é- lè- ve,

-ment;

-chè- ve Et l'as- su- re é- ter- nel- le- ment.

Et l'as- su- re é- ter- nel- le- ment.

Et l'as- su- re é- ter- nel- le- ment.

L'un tout esprit, et tout céleste

Stanza 2 of *Mon Dieu, quelle guerre cruelle!* (mm. 19–40)

Jean Racine, *Cantiques spirituels* III.2 — Jean-Baptiste Moreau

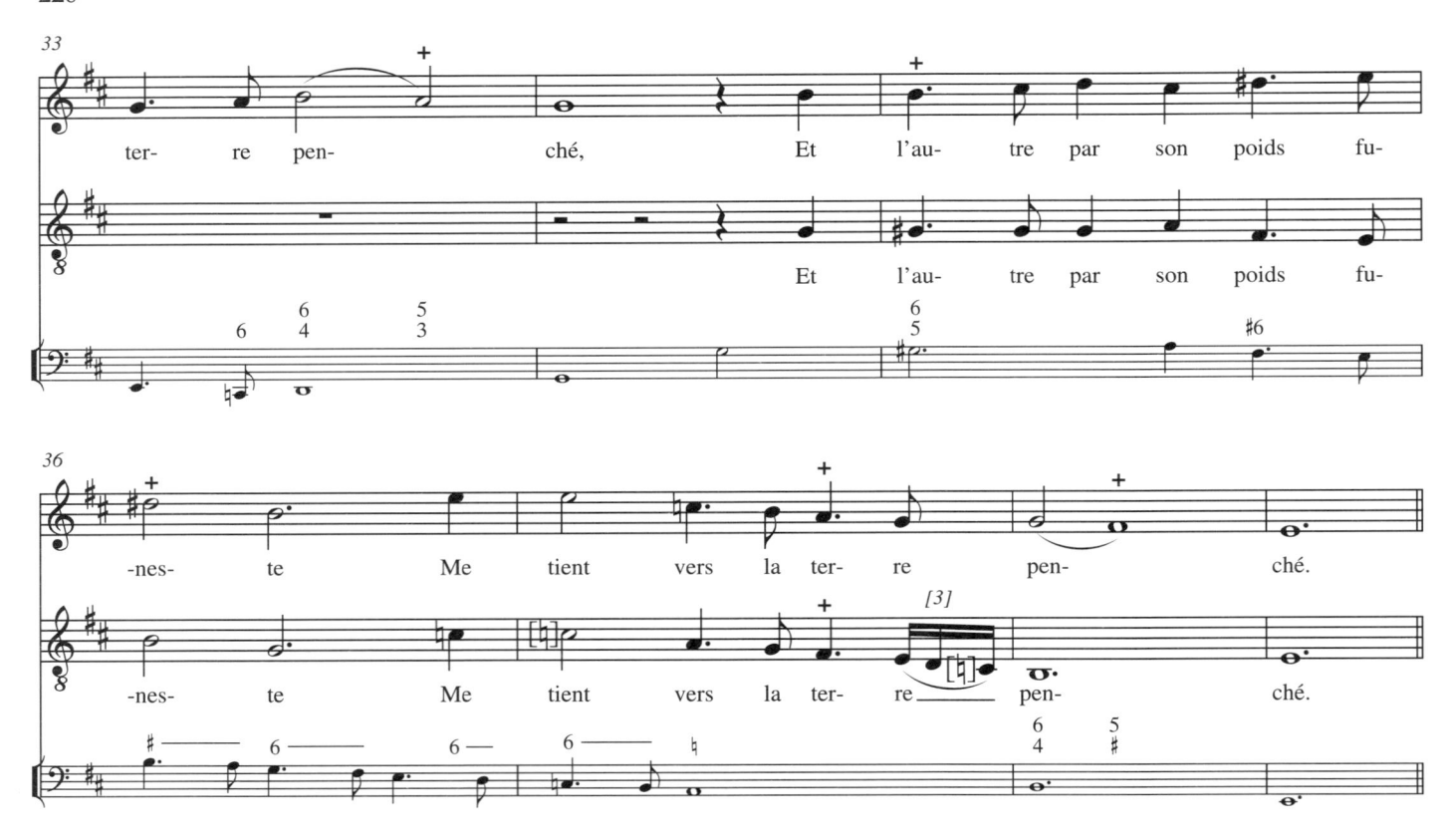

Ô grâce, ô rayon salutaire

Stanza 4 of *Mon Dieu, quelle guerre cruelle!* (mm. 59–79)

Jean Racine, *Cantiques spirituels* III.4

Jean-Baptiste Moreau

-fort Cet homme qui t'est si contrai-

-fort Cet homme qui t'est si con-trai-

-re, Fais ton es-cla-ve vo-lon-tai-re De cet es-cla-ve

-re,

de la mort, Fais ton es-cla-ve vo-lon-tai-re

Fais ton es-cla-ve vo-lon-tai-re

De cet es-cla-ve de la mort.

De cet es-cla-ve de la mort.

Infortunés que nous sommes

Stanza 3 of *Heureux qui, de la sagesse* (mm. 79–106)

Jean Racine, *Cantiques spirituels* II.3   Michel-Richard de Lalande

In- for- tu- nés que nous som- mes, Où s'é- ga- raient nos es-
-prits? Voi- là, di- ront- ils, ces hom- mes, Vils ob- jets de nos mé- pris.
-pris. Leur sain- te et pé- ni- ble vi- e Nous pa- rut u- ne fo- li-

Gravement

-e; Mais au- jour- d'hui tri- om- phants, Le ciel chan-
-te leur lou- an- ge Et Dieu lui- mê- me les ran- ge Au

103
D1
D2
B.c.
Duo
Doucement
Leur sain- te et pé- ni- ble
nom- bre de ses en- fants. Leur sain- te et pé- ni- ble
107
vi- e Nous pa- rut u- ne fo- li- e;
vi- e Nous pa- rut u- ne fo- li- e;
111
Gravement
Mais au- jour- d'hui tri- om- phants, Le ciel chan- te leur lou- an-
Mais au- jour- d'hui tri- om- phants, Le ciel chan- te leur lou- an-
116
-ge Et Dieu lui- mê- me les ran- ge Au nom- bre de ses en- fants.
-ge Et Dieu lui- mê- me les ran- ge Au nom- bre de ses en- fants.

Pour trouver un bien fragile

Stanza 4 of *Heureux qui, de la sagesse* (mm. 107–32)

Jean Racine, *Cantiques spirituels* II.4 — Michel-Richard de Lalande

225

128

D1: Dans u- ne rou- te_in- sen-

D2: -riè- re De la bien- heu- reu- se paix. Dans u- ne rou- te_in- sen-

B.c.

133

D1: -sé- e No- tre_â- me_en vain s'est las- sé- e, Sans se re- po- ser ja- mais,

D2: -sé- e No- tre_â- me_en vain s'est las- sé- e, Sans se re- po- ser ja- mais,

B.c.

138

D1: Fer- mant l'œil à la lu- miè- re Qui nous mon-

D2: Fer- mant l'œil à la lu- miè- re Qui nous mon-

B.c.

142

D1: -trait la car- riè- re De la bien- heu- reu- se paix.

D2: -trait la car- riè- re De la bien- heu- reu- se paix.

B.c.

De nos attentats injustes

Stanza 5 of *Heureux qui, de la sagesse* (mm. 133–57)

Jean Racine, *Cantiques spirituels* II.5
Michel-Richard de Lalande

149
D1
-ment, Fai- bles et tris- tes vic- ti- mes, Nous y ve- nons de nos
D2
-ment, Fai- bles et tris- tes vic- ti- mes, Nous y ve- nons de nos
B.c.
[6——] [♮5] [6] [♯6]
153
D1
cri- mes Ac- com- pa- gnés seu- le- ment. Sans a- -ment.»
D2
cri- mes Ac- com- pa- gnés seu- le- ment. Sans a- -ment.»
B.c.
[6]
1.
2.

Critical Notes

All musical excerpts in the appendix appear in their sources in fragmentary or incomplete form (see "Sources" in the critical report). The processes and materials used to complete each setting are described below under "comments." "Notes" lists rejected source readings that are not otherwise covered in the editorial methods. The initial measure numbers given in the appendix selections correspond to the initial measure numbers of the section in the main setting which they replace; subsequent measure numbering may not correspond exactly to that of the main setting. Locations within each movement are identified by measure number (M., Mm.) and part. The following abbreviations for instrumental and vocal parts are used: Fl. = Flûte/Flûte allemande, Vn. = Violon, D = Dessus, BT = Basse-taille, B = Basse, B.c. = Basse continue. Pitches are identified according to the system in which middle C is c'.

"Que je vois de Vertus" (Moreau)

Comments. The basse continue part is adapted from the main setting, with some pitches adjusted or transposed to accommodate the added voice.

Notes. Mm. 79–89, barlines occur every two beats. M. 86, D, note is g♯".

"L'Amour sur tous les dons" (Moreau)

Comments. The basse continue part for mm. 172–78 has been devised editorially, since the dessus voice part was changed from the original, and the two added parts do not conform to the original harmony. In mm. 178–87, the basse continue part is taken from the main setting.

Notes. M. 172, B, erroneous F3 clef. M. 174, D2, notes 2–4 are all 32nds. M. 176, D1, note 1 is dotted half. M. 178, D1, notes 1–2 are both g'.

"L'un tout esprit, et tout céleste" (Moreau)

Comments. No time signature is given in the source. The basse continue part is adapted from the main setting, with some pitches adjusted or transposed to accommodate the added voice.

Notes. M. 29, double barline between beats 2–3. M. 37, BT, note 4 is quarter, notes 5–7 are all 32nds.

"Ô grâce, ô rayon salutaire" (Moreau)

Comments. The basse continue part is adapted from the main setting, with some pitches adjusted or transposed to accommodate the added voice.

Notes. M. 64, D, notes 2–4 are all 32nds. M. 76, B, note 1 is quarter, notes 2–4 are all 32nds.

"Infortunés que nous sommes" (Lalande)

Comments. Adapted to incorporate the alternative duo setting of the second half of the stanza, "Leur sainte et pénible vie." The duo appears in the source directly after m. 106 of the main setting, with the following indication: "La seconde fois on peut dire la Reprise en duo comme elle est cy-aprés" (the second time, the reprise can be sung as the following duo).

"Pour trouver un bien fragile" (Lalande)

Comments. Adapted to incorporate the alternative duo setting of the second half of the stanza, "Dans une route insensée." The duo appears in the source directly after m. 132 of the main setting, with the following indication: "On peut encore repeter cette Reprise en Duo" (this reprise can be repeated as a duo).

Notes. M. 136, B.c., note 3, figures are $\frac{5}{3}$ and $\frac{7}{4}$. M. 141, B.c., note 1, figure is ♭.

"De nos attentats injustes" (Lalande)

Comments. This setting appears in the source directly after m. 132, with the following indication given above the solo setting of the same stanza beginning at m. 133: "A la place de ce couplet on peut dire le duo ci-après qui est sur les mêmes paroles" (Instead of the following couplet, one can sing the subsequent duo set to the same words).

Note. M. 133, B.c., beat 2 through m. 156, clef is C1.